DAVI

FREEDOM FOR FATHERS

Then you will know the truth and the truth will set you free.

John 8:32

Freedom for Fathers

Published by Kardo International Ministries

ISBN: 978-0-9825183-2-8

Design by Christena Ray

Kardo International Ministries
11875 West Little York #104
Houston, TX 77041
1-888-272-6972
1-713-849-9335
www.fatherwise.org

Printed in the United States of America

To Cliff, Micah, Aaron, and Benjamin

My "sons and grandson" according to covenant

WELCOME TO THIS FATHERWISE FREEDOM FOR FATHERS BIBLE STUDY!

You can use this material in one of three ways. You can get some men together at a church or in a home, and work through the material with a mentor/Bible study leader. You will begin your session with Bible study teaching and discussing your answers to the Bible study questions in the book, and then pray together using the suggestions given. You'll close your session discussing the Parenting Skills and using the discussion questions in this book.

Or you may do this study on your own while your wife studies my wife's book, *Freedom for Mothers*. The two of you can use the weekly Discussion Questions to work on your marriage and parenting skills together.

The third way to use this book is to do it individually. If you are a single dad or a man still waiting on your wife to respond to God, this may be a good option. Although being in a group is better, we pray the Lord will speak through His Word and Spirit as you study this material.

If you are participating in a group study, the first meeting will be a time to get acquainted with the men in your small discussion group by answering Questions For Group Discussion to familiarize yourself with the course and how it works and to study the first lesson. When you go home, you'll read through the daily devotionals in preparation for the next meeting. Please note there are five days of devotionals for the first five days of the week, then a Weekend Study lesson to be completed on either Saturday or Sunday. It will take an investment of time on your part, but the rewards of daily study time to listen and learn as the Word and the Spirit teach you are worth it!

Overview of the Next Eight Weeks
FULLNESS AND FREEDOM FOR MEN

In the next eight weeks, we are going to be taking a journey in God's Word to discover the freedom we can experience as men to be all we can be. This journey begins with a look inside and ends at the foot of the cross. You may have never experienced Jesus the way you will during the next few weeks. During this study you will learn:

Week 1: The Principle of the Vine
FILLING YOUR LIFE FROM THE POWER SOURCE

To function completely, you've got to be empowered for the tasks at hand. In Week 1, we'll discover that the power source for getting your personal needs met is Jesus, the only one who can truly meet those needs. This is the vital first step to being a successful man, husband, and father.

Weeks 2&3: The Principle of the Branch
RUNNING OUT OF STEAM

Most of us go to all the wrong places to try to get our needs met for significance and security. We end up discouraged, depressed, and distraught. In Weeks 2 and 3 of this book, we will identify what the Bible has to say about the roadblocks we face in becoming empowered to be godly husbands and fathers.

Weeks 4&5: The Principle of the Shears
THE ULTIMATE SOLUTION

The answer to our deepest need is simpler than most of us think. God's plan for our freedom and fulfillment is not complicated, but it is costly. Weeks 4 and 5 will take us on a journey to the cross—the only place where troubles can end and life can begin.

Week 6: The Principle of the Bud

The Transformed Life

We want to be a men who exhibit love, joy, peace, patience, kindness, goodness, faithfulness, gentleness and self-control in every situation. But in reality we sometimes disappoint ourselves. We can't do it on our own. It requires someone to do it for us...someone whose love is always pure and whose thoughts are always wise. In Week 6, we will discover how to begin the process of allowing Christ to renew our hearts and minds and to live His life in us, through us, and for us. This is how fulfillment and freedom can finally be ours.

Weeks 7&8: The Principle of the Fruit

Keeping the Bucket Full

Now that I know where to plug into Christ's power source, I want to stay connected. I want to continuously express peace, patience, and self-control. That's a tall order. It requires setting our minds on Christ and being equipped to engage in spiritual warfare. Those are the topics of Weeks 7 and 8—the powerful conclusion to our study.

Are you ready to have true meaning in your life? Are you ready to experience freedom in your work and wholeness in your family relationships? Are you ready to be fully whole and clean and pure? I must tell you there is a cost. The process is simple, but expensive. In fact, it will cost you your very life. But in return, you will experience life as it was meant to be lived—with all the joy, peace, and patience you can possibly contain. You will "run and not grow weary, you will walk and not grow faint."

If you come to God hungry and ready to be filled up with what He can give you, you will be amazed at what He will do. He will do more for you than you can imagine. I cannot promise that your work situation will immediately resolve and that your marriage and parenting will be perfectly in tune after this study. But I can tell you that if you allow God access to your heart during the next eight weeks and ask Him to fill you with all that you need for your circumstances, He will do more than you can imagine.

I'm praying for you as you read this book. I'm praying that your life will be intersected with God's life in a powerful and meaningful way and that you will know the truth that will make you free.

David Glenn

ADDITIONAL RESOURCES AND OPPORTUNITIES

We would like to encourage you to visit our website at www.fatherwise.org. Our website is continually updated and provides information about the following:

Bible Studies:

Information regarding all of the FatherWise Bible studies including excerpts from our books.

On-line store:

View and order the FatherWise and MotherWise materials including translations in many different languages. Some of the translations available include: Spanish, Indonesian, Korean, and Russian. Please check our website on an ongoing basis for new and updated translations. To receive a discount on your next online purchase, enter this code at checkout: FFM09 (for a discount on *Freedom For Mothers* products) or FFF09 (for a discount on *Freedom For Fathers* products)

FatherWise News Updates:

Read about what's coming up and the latest news in FatherWise and MotherWise.

International News:

View the International locations where FatherWise is currently.

Missions:

FatherWise would love to partner with your church or ministry in taking the materials on a mission trip. View this area on the website for more information.

Prayer:

Join our prayer team or submit a prayer request.

About David Glenn:

More about our author, speaker and founder, David Glenn.

Conferences:

We can partner with you to provide conferences centered around the following Bible Study topics:

Wisdom for Fathers and *Freedom for Fathers*

FatherWise Group List

Mentor/Bible Study Teacher

Name: ____

Family's names and ages: _______________________________

____

____

____

____

Address: ____

Phone: (_____) - ______ - ______

Prayer/Discussion Group

Name: ____

Family's names and ages: _______________________________

____

____

____

____

Address: ____

Phone: (_____) - ______ - ______

Name: ____

Family's names and ages: _______________________________

____

____

____

____

Address: ____

Phone: (_____) - ______ - ______

Name: ____

Family's names and ages: ________________________________

____

____

____

____

Address: ____

Phone: (_____) - ______ - ______

Name: ____

Family's names and ages: ________________________________

____

____

____

____

Address: ____

Phone: (_____) - ______ - ______

Name: ____

Family's names and ages: ________________________________

____

____

____

____

Address: ____

Phone: (_____) - ______ - ______

Name: ____

Family's names and ages: _______________________________

____

____

____

____

Address: ____

Phone: (_____) - ______ - ______

Name: ____

Family's names and ages: _______________________________

____

____

____

____

Address: ____

Phone: (_____) - ______ - ______

Name: ____

Family's names and ages: _______________________________

____

____

____

____

Address: ____

Phone: (_____) - ______ - ______

FatherWise Group Prayer Guidelines

1. If your FatherWise ministry has many age groups of men, break into small groups of 5-6 for prayer time each week.

2. We recommend that prayer time be observed before the Parenting Skills discussion time. Experience has taught us that it is difficult to stop discussion and begin prayer time. Please keep prayer requests limited to yourself and your immediate family [wife and children]. While we realize that prayer for our extended family and friends is very important, FatherWise time should be focused on your immediate family.

3. Please remember that what you discuss in prayer time is very personal. We ask that the requests lifted up in class be kept confidential within the group.

4. When you pray as a group, pray conversationally. Let one man share a request for his family and then all the men in the group should pray over that one request. Then the next man can share his request for the group to pray over until all the men in the group have had an opportunity to share a request.

5. Prayer time together is a vital part of FatherWise. We look forward to all that God will do in it and through it!

WEEK 1

POWER SOURCE: LIFE IN THE VINE

For a man to be able to give love to his wife and children, first he must have his own needs met. Many men try to get those needs met from achievements. Is that the answer?

FatherWise Group Prayer Requests

The first person in the group will share a one sentence prayer request about his wife or his children. Each person in the group will pray a one sentence prayer over that request before moving on to the next person's request. The group will continue in this way until everyone has prayed over each request.

DAY 1

POWER SOURCE: LIFE IN THE VINE

BEGIN WITH PRAYER

Ask God to show you His heart for being a godly father. Be still and quiet before Him.

You probably looked forward to becoming a father, but perhaps the pressures of providing for a growing family's needs are beginning to mount up. Children require major adjustments in your life, especially in your marriage. Issues of the children's discipline and character development arise. It is expensive both in time and money to raise good kids. Thankfully, you and your wife don't have to tackle the job alone. There is someone to come alongside you. His name is Jesus.

But Jesus did not come to just help you be a man, husband and father. He didn't come to just put His arm around you like the Big Guy in the Sky and give you a little pep talk. He came to do the work for you, in you and through you. That is totally different than pulling yourself up by the bootstraps, trying very hard and then asking Jesus to bless you. Jesus wants to bless you by filling your life with His life so He can accomplish His purposes on the earth through you.

In the next eight weeks, we will journey with God, asking Him to remove roadblocks in our lives so we can be free to be the men He designed us to be. God wants us to be godly men even more than we want it for ourselves.

Probably every man reading this has fantasized about being a Superman or Macho Man or hero of some sort. That's not all bad, Guys. God made us to be strong and independent — to be the providers and protectors for our homes. The problem comes when we think we can do it all on our own.

In JOHN 15:5, Jesus tells His disciples, *"I am the vine, you are the branches; he who abides in me, and I in him, he bears much fruit; for apart from me you can do nothing."*

Nothing? As we say in Texas, "That's a zero with the rim knocked off." I cannot truly do my job as a husband, father, or at my workplace apart from His vine-life in me.

LIFE IS IN THE SAP OF THE VINE. Grapes form when sap so fills the vine and branches that it pops out of the branch as fruit. That's how your life is when you abide in Christ. The fruit of His Spirit (peace, patience, and all the rest) will simply flow out of you when you're really connected to Christ. It won't require self-effort; it will happen naturally as a result of abiding in the Vine life of Jesus.

But first we must ask a basic question. Are you connected to Christ? Have you made a personal commitment to Jesus, making Him Lord of your life? If not, this is where to begin. Turn to Sabbath Study at the end of this week's study and read the passages there.

If you have already made this crucial first step in receiving God's love and power, then you may be asking: "How do I stay connected to Christ by "abiding in the Vine?" What does that look like? How does attachment to Christ affect my marriage? My parenting?"

THE EMPTY BUCKET: We all have a place inside ourselves that I call an "empty bucket." It is the place that needs to be filled with security and significance. What would fill your inner bucket? What would make you feel satisfied, secure, and happy right now?

In our "empty buckets," we need to know we are secure and "safe." Many men may hate to admit it, but we all want love and acceptance and the feeling of security. While financial security probably tops our lists, we also want secure relationships in a wife we can count on, kids we are proud of, and friends we can turn to.

We also need to know that we have value, that we are significant. We need to receive a "medal" in something important to us. We want to know our lives count for something. These basic needs of security and significance are not optional. They are needs that must be met.

PHILIPPIANS 4:19 says, *"And my God will meet all your needs according to his glorious riches in Christ Jesus." All life is in Jesus, and He alone is able to meet ALL our needs without ever letting us down or disappointing us."*

So today, spend a few moments asking God to meet every need for security and significance you can think of. Just lay them out before Him honestly. Then, wait and watch Him begin to work!

Lord Jesus, I want Your Vine-life to flow through me. I trust You to meet every true need I have for security and significance. I pray this in the name of Jesus. Amen.

TIPS FOR DAD

Make sure the kids know that (after the Lord) their mom is first in your life. Take her on dates without the kids as often as possible. Continue to "win her over" as you did before marriage. By loving her sacrificially as we are commanded (EPHESIANS 5), your children will see how important she is and will respect her authority over them.

DAY 2

POWER SUPPLY

BEGIN BY READING

Psalm 81:10: *"I am the LORD your God, who brought you up out of Egypt. Open wide your mouth and I will fill it."* In prayer, ask God to fill you today.

The word "fill" in Psalm 81:10 is the Hebrew word *mala.*[1] One of the meanings of that word is "to satisfy." If we open our hearts to the Lord, He promises to satisfy our longings. As men, we often have lofty aspirations and intense desires. We also carry heavy responsibilities that can weigh us down.

You may have started your career or family with high hopes, only to become discouraged. No matter how wonderful (or horrible) your job, wife, or kids may be, they are not God. They simply cannot meet all the needs of your heart.

Read John 15:1-5. *The first lesson I must learn is that Christ is the Vine, I am not. He is God, and I am not.* Let that sink in. Are you tempted to play God in your own life?

Jesus did not come to help you with your life. He came to *be* your life, and that is very different. He did not just come to be your Savior and Lord. He came to be your life! Jesus told us the secret to bearing fruit: we must abide in Him and He must abide in us. That means being grafted into His Vine-life. Grafting involves cutting both the vine and the new branch. The life-giving centers of each (the *cambium*) are matched perfectly and tied together securely. The vine sends up shoots into the new branch, and the new branch sends down shoots into the vine. Life begins to flow. Fruit is formed. The vine and the branch have become one.[2]

Read ROMANS 11:16-18 in your Bible. Here, Paul describes the grafting in of the Gentiles, the *"wild olive branch,"* into the rich root of the olive tree, the life of the Lord Jesus. We partake of His life because He has mercifully grafted us in.

The cambium of our hearts, our inmost self, must become one with His heart. We must be tied together firmly. And in the growth process, I must remain still in Him so that my roots can go deep into Him and He can abide deeply in me.

How do you abide? You begin by reaching up to Him in prayer, and He pours His life into you through His Word dwelling in you. As you take in more of His Word and obey it, you will begin to see His fruit borne out in you. Acknowledging that you can't do everything and only He can is the first step to really being free.

Father, I offer my emptiness to You, asking You to fill it with Yourself. I truly desire to abide in You and want You to abide in me. Enable me to receive Your life in all its fullness. I admit I have used other things and people to try to get my needs met, but today I am turning to You. I love you, Lord. In Jesus' name. Amen.

TIPS FOR DAD

Let Jesus use your hands and feet to bless someone today. Offer to help your wife with the kids or the dishes. For adolescents, put a note on their bed or mirror reminding them that you love them and are praying for them today. Then go to their bed when they aren't home and kneel down and pray for them.

DAY 3

WHO POWERS THE "REAL" YOU

BEGIN WITH PRAYER

Enter into God's presence with thanksgiving. Thank Him for being in control of the universe and in control of your life. Acknowledge to Him that He alone is your source of life. Ask God to prepare your heart and mind for what He wants to teach you today and to remove any barriers that would prevent you from understanding these great truths He has given us as believers.

LIVING "IN" HIM

Read I JOHN 3:23-24.

23 Now John also was baptizing at Aenon near Salim, because there was plenty of water, and people were constantly coming to be baptized.
24 (This was before John was put in prison.)

John explains what it means to "abide in Christ" when he gives us these two commandments to follow – to believe in the name of Jesus and to love one another. Obedience is critical to abiding. We can't go our own way and still be connected to Christ's life. We can't have it both ways. We must connect to the Vine. And what are we to obey? The law of love. We are to love the Lord with all our hearts and minds and souls and love our neighbors the same as we love ourselves.

Read II PETER 1:2-3 in your Bible.

2 Grace and peace be yours in abundance through the knowledge of God and of Jesus our Lord.

3 His divine power has given us everything we need for life and godliness through our knowledge of him who called us by his own glory and goodness.

It tells us that Jesus has called us by His own glory and excellence to have everything we need to live this life and to live it in a godly lifestyle. It is through the true knowledge of Him that we will have His life operating in us.

Now let's make this very practical. Could Jesus manage your job? Could He discipline your children firmly and fairly with perfect consistency? Could He relate to your wife with unconditional love and acceptance, without being demanding or selfish? Yes, of course He could. Can you do all those things all the time? No, of course you can't.

If you are a believer, you have the life of the resurrected Lord Jesus Christ operating on the inside of you. He is able to do whatever He has called you to do. He has not asked you to do it. He knows you can't. What He wants is to accomplish His purpose and His will in you and through you. That is very different from "helping" you do it. Do you see?

The task of being a godly husband and father is over your head. I don't care how many degrees in rocket science or engineering you have. Being a father is bigger than you are. If you don't know that, you probably haven't been a dad for very long. The only person who is accomplished at the awesome task of fatherhood is our Heavenly Father. He sent His Son to explain a father's heart to us and sent His Spirit to transfrom us into the men we should be.

Lord, I want You to take over the controls of my life. I can't do it. It is too hard and too complicated for me to do well. I know that You are able to accomplish every task for me and through me. I now trust You to do that. I pray this in the name of Jesus Christ. Amen.

TIPS FOR DAD

When our children get frustrated and direct that anger at us, it's very easy to lash out and escalate the situation. Begin practicing what you learned today about Jesus being your life. When you find yourself in the middle of turmoil with your child, call a "time out." Let him know you need to collect your thoughts and pray before you talk to him, because you don't want to say something you will regret. Take a few moments to ask Jesus to be your wisdom and discernment in that circumstance. Ask Him to direct your attitudes and your actions toward your child. Then, if it's time to mete out firm discipline, you'll know it. If it's time to sit on the couch and listen to your child express all of what's on his mind, you'll know that too. I've been amazed at the insight I receive "on the spot" when I've stopped to pray before acting.

DAY 4

THE POWER OF SIGNIFICANT TRUTHS

BEGIN WITH PRAYER

Ask the Father to speak to you clearly through His Word today, and to bind your mind to His will and purposes.

Growing up, I was an over-achiever to make up for a low self image. But even when I was "achieving" all on my list, I still felt I wasn't quite good enough. I feared failure; I feared rejection; I feared FEAR! As the challenges grew greater through the years, so did my fear. I felt more pressure to perform at work, and the pressure to be the "all-around great husband and dad" was just too much. The more I tried, the more powerless I felt. That's when God began showing me that He created me with these needs so that He could fill them through His life in me.

Read Ephesians 3:14-21 in your Bible.

14 For this reason I kneel before the Father, 15 from whom his whole family in heaven and on earth derives its name. 16 I pray that out of his glorious riches he may strengthen you with power through his Spirit in your inner being, 17 so that Christ may dwell in your hearts through faith. And I pray that you, being rooted and established in love, 18 may have power, together with all the saints, to grasp how wide and long and high and deep is the love of Christ, 19 and to know this love that surpasses knowledge—that you may be filled to the measure of all the fullness of God.

20 Now to him who is able to do immeasurably more than all we ask or imagine, according to his power that is at work within us, 21 to him be glory in the church and in Christ Jesus throughout all generations, for ever and ever! Amen.

VERSES 14-15. By calling God *"Father,"* Paul establishes that before we can receive Christ's love, we must be part of God's family. I don't have to rely on my achievements to know the truth about myself. I can ask the Source that's always true, my Heavenly Father.

VERSE 16. My inner man may feel so weak and full of fear that I'm incapable of receiving Christ's life and love. So the first thing Jesus does is to strengthen my inner man. The word *power* in verse 16 is the Greek word *dunamis,* which means "miraculous power, strength, violence, mighty (wonderful) work."[3] Jesus strengthens me with His mighty, dynamic, dynamite-like power so that He may dwell—or live permanently in residence—in my heart, to fill up all the holes and gaps.

VERSE 17. Christ enables me to be "rooted and grounded" in His empowering love. *Rooted* means "made stable."[4] Think back to JOHN 15:4. We need abiding roots going deep into His love to hold us steady in life's circumstances, as well as the constant feeding from that same Source. *Grounded* means "to lay a foundation."[5] When our Houston home needed foundation repair, men put it on pillars on solid rock far beneath the surface. That's what Jesus intends for your life: to be rooted in His love and founded on the solid, never-shifting rock of His love. This is the purpose for His "dwelling in your heart by faith" – to supply your every need. His message to you is LOVE and SIGNIFICANCE.

VERSES 18-20. Jesus comes to dwell in your heart so that you will *comprehend* and *know* His love. *Comprehend* means "to take eagerly, seize and possess."[6] *Know* means "to be sure, to understand to be resolved."[7] These verses could be rewritten: "(That you) may be able to eagerly grasp with all Christians the breadth, length, height and depth and to know for sure the love of Christ..." This is the message Jesus is sending you: you are loved, accepted, and secure. Even better, this love surpasses knowledge. It is so vast your brain can't take it all in. If that weren't enough, this big love of God is for a specific purpose: to top off your emotional tank. The Greek word for *filled up* means "crammed full, leveled off, satisfied."[8] That's enough love to fill every crevice of your heart. You have no burden, failure, or fear that Christ's love can't fill beyond your wildest dreams, above all you could even ask.

You cannot give away what you do not possess. Your family needs your unconditional love. But to give it, you must first receive love yourself. You need a full bucket of His empowering love to be a dad. And it is available to you.

Lord, please open my capacity to receive Your love and acceptance. I want to know that Your love is enough even when others let me down. Teach me all this in my inner man. In Jesus' name. Amen.

TIPS FOR DAD

A father is to imitate his Heavenly Father's love for his kids. Find practical ways to show love to your kids. Rock small tykes. If they're older, have a date with girls or take sons to a game. If your kids are already out of the nest, give them a call or an email just to say, "How's it going?" and "I love you." Making time for them shows they're special to you.

DAY 5

POWER LIVING

BEGIN WITH PRAYER

Ask the Lord Jesus to root and ground you in His life, and to allow you to comprehend and know His love that goes beyond what you can understand with your mind.

Let me give you a word picture of what it's like for Christ to live His life in you. Imagine you are a scarecrow standing in a field. The "birds of prey" are after your family and you can do nothing about it. You are lifeless and powerless to protect them. But the farmer comes along and removes all the old straw, puts on your scarecrow's clothes and goes out into the field for you. The birds of prey don't stand a chance of getting to your family, because now the scarecrow has come to life!

Read JOHN 14:20 in your Bible and draw a diagram of four concentric circles in the margin of this page. Label the largest circle "God," the next "Jesus," the next "me," and the smallest "Jesus." Do you see the liberating truth of this verse? Jesus is on the inside of you and He is on the outside of you and that's the only two sides you have!

Jesus is filling the inside of us so He can handle our lives for us! And nothing can get to us that hasn't been filtered by His love. So if He allows a circumstance to come to us, He will then handle it. It is our job is to trust Him with it. His job is to do the work. There is nothing He cannot do (LUKE 1:37).

Have you noticed that you can't keep God's laws all on your own? If you're trying hard, you might do well for a while, but you don't have any real staying power. God never intended for you to keep His commands apart from Him. That's why Jesus came to earth. You couldn't keep His covenant, so He came, died and rose again to live in you... to do it for you.

Read JOHN 11:25 and COLOSSIANS 3:4 in your Bible. *Jesus did not come to help you with your life. He came to be your life.* Let that sink in. There is a radical difference between the two. Without His life flowing through you, you're incapable of being the man you know you should be (JOHN 15:5).

In your Bible, circle the word "fullness" in the following verses. JOHN 1:16; EPHESIANS 1:22-23; and EPHESIANS 3:19. Even when I don't *feel* His power, I must base my faith on the truth of God's Word that His power fills me up and is present and available to me.

Lord, I want You to be my power source, my life. Reveal Yourself to me day by day so I can fully understand the truth. Amen.

TIPS FOR DAD

One of the strongest messages *Promise Keepers* has given men is the message of Proverbs 27:17, "*As iron sharpens iron, so one man sharpens another.*" Having at least one other man to share your struggles and victories with is one of the greatest gifts a man can have. My prayer partners have been one of my greatest sources of encouragement and strength. They've prayed me through some tough times. If you don't have an accountability/prayer group, begin asking God to provide one for you.

WEEKEND STUDY

GETTING CONNECTED TO THE VINE

BEGIN BY READING

If you want to connect yourself to Jesus for the first time in your life, start by reading ACTS 16:31: *"Believe in the Lord Jesus, and you will be saved — you and your household."* To trust God fully you must trust Him through Jesus Christ, His Son. In JOHN 14:6, Jesus says of Himself, *"I am the way and the truth and the life. No one comes to the Father except through me."* Turning your life over to Jesus is the only way to have a relationship with God. You must go through Jesus. Ask God to speak to you as you explore this truth in the book of ROMANS.

THE ROMAN ROAD TO SALVATION

ROMANS 3:23 *"For all have sinned and fall short of the glory of God."*

ROMANS 6:23 *"For the wages of sin is death, but the free gift of God is eternal life in Christ Jesus our Lord."*

ROMANS 5:8 *"But God demonstrates His own love toward us, in that while we were yet sinners, Christ died for us."*

ROMANS 10:9-10 *"That if you confess with your mouth Jesus as Lord, and believe in your heart that God raised Him from the dead, you shall be saved; ...for with the heart man believes, resulting in righteousness, and with the mouth he confesses, resulting in salvation."*

ROMANS 10:13 *"For whoever will call on the name of the Lord will be saved."*

To have a relationship with God — to become "born again" — you must:

First, admit you are a sinner and need a relationship with Jesus Christ to save you from everlasting condemnation. Second, admit and confess your sins to God. Repent, or make an about face, turning from sin to God. Third, ask Jesus to save you by His grace, to come in to your life and become Lord of your life. By that I mean He is to rule your life...His agenda is your agenda.

IF YOU ARE READY, PRAY A PRAYER LIKE THIS:

"Lord Jesus, I am a sinner and I admit it. I am confessing this to You today. Forgive me of my sins. I want your death on the cross to pay the penalty for my sins. I turn now from my sin, and I turn to You. Save me and have mercy on me, Lord. Be my Master and my Lord. You alone are my God. In Jesus' name I pray. Amen."

If you prayed that prayer from your heart, the angels are rejoicing! You are now God's child! You've just been born into a new family! NOW you have the power source to become the kind of father that will bless your children.

Write today's date or the date of your own experience with trusting God for the first time. ____________/______/______________

Call on your pastor or a Christian friend and share this important decision. You need to tell someone about your new faith!

"Whoever acknowledges me before men, I will also acknowledge him before my Father in heaven" (MATTHEW 10:32).

MY POSITION IN CHRIST One of the most in influential books in helping me understand the vine life of Jesus is *Handbook to Happiness*, by Dr. Charles Solomon.[9] In this book, he uses mathematical illustrations that really opened my eyes to this great truth of Jesus' vine-life in me. The Lord used this book to literally transform my thinking about my new identity in Him. It enabled me to see how Jesus could undertake for me and through me, the mission of my life, my marriage and my responsibility as a father. I want to share it with you.

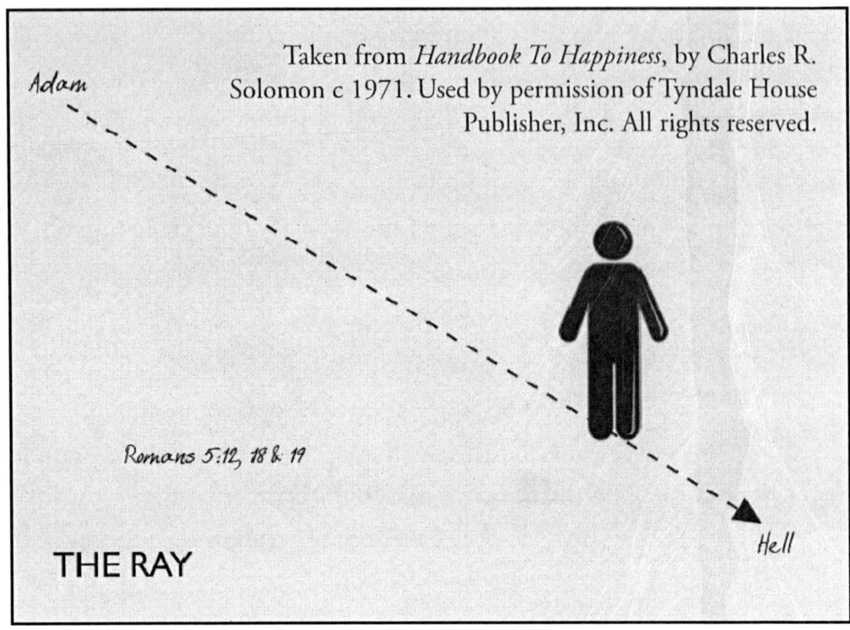

The ray represents Adam's life. God created Adam at a definite point in time. Adam sinned, so his life's "ray" is pointing down toward hell. All people born on the earth are born into his family, the family of man. Before I became a Christian, I was like a dot on that ray.

I CORINTHIANS 15:21-22 says: "*For since by a man came death, by a man also came the resurrection of the dead. For as in Adam all die, so also in Christ all shall be made alive.*"

As a member of Adam's family, we are doomed to hell. We will all die eternally. But there is good news.

A Line: Now think about a line. A line in math is a string of points along a plane that go for infinity in both directions. This line represents the lifeline of Jesus Christ. His life goes forever in the past and forever in the future.

Read HEBREWS 1:6-12 and JOHN 17:24 in your Bible. The lifeline of Jesus intersects the line of Adam. When we recognize that we are

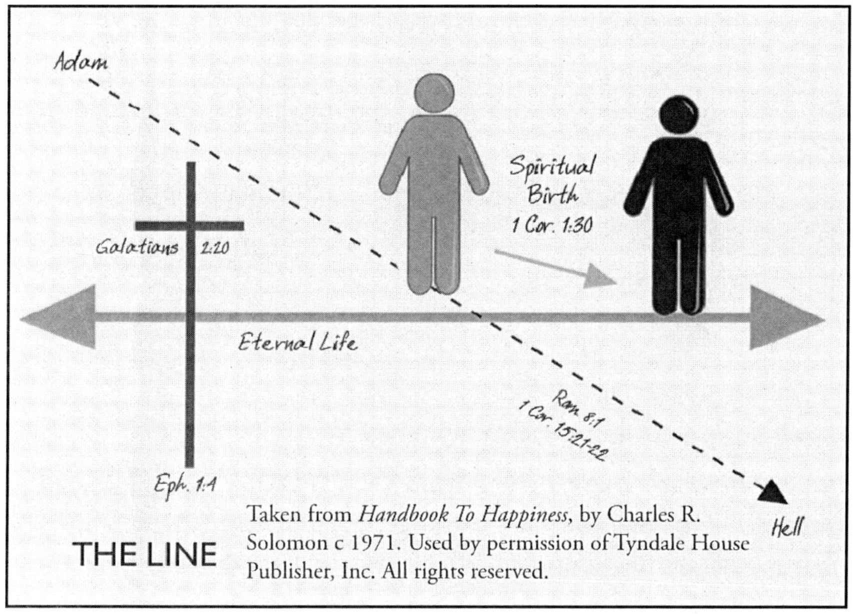

Taken from *Handbook To Happiness*, by Charles R. Solomon c 1971. Used by permission of Tyndale House Publisher, Inc.

doomed to hell because our sins deserve it, choose to repent of our sins, and ask Jesus Christ to be our indwelling Lord and Master, we "jump" from the line of Adam to the life line of the Lord Jesus. We have a new identity – we now share His life! His life is our life!

Read EPHESIANS 1:3-13. Do you see all the incredible riches that belong to you when you are "in Him" on that eternal life line? You share His life. You are in covenant relationship with Him, so that all He has, He gives to you. He has given you every spiritual blessing in the heavenly places, adoption as His child, redemption through His blood, the forgiveness of your sins, has made known to you the mystery of His will, an inheritance to be the praise of His glory, and you've been sealed with the Holy Spirit. All this and more we receive because our lives are "in" Him.

You have absolutely everything you need. This is the truth! It does not depend on how you feel about it to be the truth. It is true because God said it. I may feel empty or stressed in my "feeler." But with my "chooser," I choose to believe the truth from God's Word that I have everything I need for this day. I have every spiritual blessing. I have enough love because I have God and He is love. I have joy because His life is in me and His life is joyous in all circumstances. I have peace because He is my peace. My peace does not depend on my circumstances. My peace depends on His life flowing though me. I can choose as an act of my will to live by His life in me, not by the swirling circumstances around me.

Your "feeler" takes input from the circumstances and panics. Your "thinker" takes input from the circumstances and begins to try to solve the problem—even if it's unsolvable! Your "chooser" must decide whether life will be lived from the input of the "feeler" or the "thinker" or it may take the third option. It can decide to submit to the life of Jesus operating within (Colossians 3:3-4).

Notes

[1] *Strong's Exhaustive Concordance, Greek Dictionary of the New Testament,* Number 1411, p. 24. Used by permission of Thomas Nelson, Inc.

[2] *World Book 1985*, Vol. G, pp. 288-290

[3] *Strong's Exhaustive Concordance, Greek Dictionary of the New Testament,* Number 1492, p. 62. Used by permission of Thomas Nelson, Inc.

[4] Ibid., Number 2311, p. 36

[5] Ibid., Number 2638, p. 40

[6] Ibid., Number 1097, p. 20

[7] Ibid., Number 4137, p. 58

[8] Ibid., Number 4492, p. 63

[9] *Handbook to Happiness,* Dr. Charles Solomon, Living Studies, Tyndale House, 1971, 1983, 1999, pp. 67, 69, 71.

WEEK 2

THE PRINCIPLE OF THE BRANCH: THE ROOT OF THE PROBLEM

If I'm a Christian, and Jesus is living on the inside of me, then why can't I always live just like Jesus on a continual basis? What is the tourniquet on my heart that keeps me from being a consistent godly husband and father?

FatherWise Group Prayer Requests

The first person in the group will share a one sentence prayer request about his wife or his children. Each person in the group will pray a one sentence prayer over that request before moving on to the next person's request. The group will continue in this way until everyone has prayed over each request.

DAY 1

THE BIG "I"

BEGIN WITH PRAYER

Ask God to search you. Try you and see if there is any hurtful way in you, and "lead you in the way everlasting" (Psalm 139:23-24).

I don't want to tell you how to patch up your role as a husband and father, to pour new information into your old thought processes. If I did, you'd be right back to your old mistakes and habits shortly after you put down this book. No, I have something much more effective to offer you.

Read Matthew 9:16-17 in your Bible.

16 "No one sews a patch of unshrunk cloth on an old garment, for the patch will pull away from the garment, making the tear worse. 17 Neither do men pour new wine into old wineskins. If they do, the skins will burst, the wine will run out and the wineskins will be ruined. No, they pour new wine into new wineskins, and both are preserved."

Here, Jesus gives us the secret to being a successful man. It's not a quick fix, instant approach. It is a completely new way of thinking and living.

Jesus uses the picture of an old garment and old wineskin to illustrate our minds and hearts. Even if we "sew" a "patch" of His Word onto our old thought patterns, it will tear when "washed" in the swirling waters of life. The new and old can't work together. We need an entirely new garment. We need new wineskins—new ways of thinking—to contain the new wine of Jesus' powerful life within us. To be a great dad, you not only need the new wine of God's Word, but also a new wineskin to contain it, a new garment to wear. You must be transformed by the renewing of your mind (ROMANS 12:2).

Sadly, many of us have adopted just enough of the Christian life to keep us from going to hell. We tip our hats to God and then go on about our business until we get into trouble. But we've missed the whole point. We've settled for mediocrity at best, failure at worst. We were created to live in victory, joy, confidence, and love. Don't accept less!

This week and next, we must make a choice: to live on our own terms or on God's, to live in the "flesh" or the "Spirit." The choice is yours, as are the consequences of that choice.

A father's choices affect the lives of his children in profound ways. Our decision to live "according to the flesh" or "according to the Spirit" will affect not only our children's lives, but also the lives of our descendants...to the third and fourth generations. Are you ready to take this adventure to get in on God's great design? Do you want to be a blessing to your children and the generations to come? Then let's begin the study of life in the "flesh" and life in the "Spirit."

Read JUDGES 21:25 in your Bible.
25 In those days Israel had no king; everyone did as he saw fit.

This is the last verse in this sad book about Israel during a particularly black period of their history. It is a definition of life in the "flesh:" *"Everyone did what was right in his own eyes."* Everyone was living according to his own "flesh" instead of in the "Spirit."

ISAIAH 53:6 says, *"each of us has turned to his own way."* Frank Sinatra's song epitomized what it's like to live in the "flesh." He sang, "I did it my way...." When I live according to what pleases me, satisfies me, exalts me, I am living in the "flesh."

In *Heart's Cry*, J. K. Dean describes "flesh" as a tourniquet.[1] A tourniquet cuts off the flow. If you have a tourniquet on your spirit quenching the flow of Christ's life, you're in trouble. Your emptiness can't be filled from the source designed to fill it. And you can't be a channel of His life to others. Unless you abide in Him, you can do nothing.

Lord Jesus, forgive me when I have chosen to live "my way" instead of Yours. Teach me what it means to live in the Spirit with my family. In Your name I pray. Amen.

TIPS FOR DAD

One of the ways to really love your wife is to help her. If she needs you to help clean up, pick up your clothes and do another chore or two. Make sure your kids cooperate with her in keeping their rooms/bathrooms clean the way she likes the house to appear.

DAY 2

F-L-E-S-H

BEGIN WITH PRAYER

Sit quietly for a moment. Ask the Father to work in a powerful way in your heart all through this week. Ask Him to keep working even when you get uncomfortable!

Read JOHN 6:63.

63 The Spirit gives life; the flesh counts for nothing. The words I have spoken to you are spirit and they are life.

The Spirit gives life and is contrasted with the flesh. Walking in the flesh brings about death...death to relationships, death to peace, death to love, death to joy. It's just not worth it! My mother-in-law shared an acrostic with me that describes flesh:

F - following

L - long

E - established

S - self-centered

H- habits

Read GALATIANS 6:8.

8 The one who sows to please his sinful nature, from that nature will reap destruction; the one who sows to please the Spirit, from the Spirit will reap eternal life.

I used to read these Scripture passages and think references to "flesh" must mean murder, lying, stealing—that kind of thing—but when our girls were teens, I began to see my own negative patterns. My inadequacies as a husband and father began to prove that I had lots of "fleshy" attitudes that needed changing.

One of the greatest truths I have learned is: *Self-revelation comes before God-revelation.* When God began to reveal my fleshy areas, then I began to see what He wanted to do to change my life. I could finally cooperate with Him, allowing Him to do the necessary surgery in my heart to get rid of flesh so the Spirit could work through me.

One of the best working descriptions of flesh I have read is "getting what I want, when I want it, the way I want it!" Notice the key word "I." A great one-word description of flesh is SELF. In fact, "flesh" spelled backwards without the "h" is "self." It is *I, my, me,* and *mine.* Flesh exhibits self-gratification—it pulls in to satisfy, and it exhibits self-legislation—it reaches out to control.

If I father my children in the flesh instead of in the Spirit, it will be defective. I will be grasping to satisfy my personal needs in my own way at the expense of others—including my children. I will be concentrating on controlling people and situations to get my needs met...the need for quiet, the need for privacy, the need to get my work done, the need for people to leave my things alone... you get the picture. When "fleshy" attitudes are the primary motivators for my behavior as a husband and father, my wife and my children will suffer.

Our daughter Stephanie had only been married eight weeks when she told us the sad story of one of her newlywed friends. The couple was already in big trouble. Stephanie said, "You can't be selfish and be married. It just doesn't work." Denise and I thought those were insightful words coming from one so newly married. (Inside we were saying, *Yes! She's got it!*)

Stephanie is right. You can't be selfish and have a good marriage. And you can't be selfish and be a good dad. There is just no way around it. We need to let go of flesh and walk in the Spirit.

Lord, I see where I have been trying to get my needs met from people, possessions, and achievements. I've controlled my family to get my needs met. Set me free, Lord to be the man, husband, and father You designed me to be. Take away all my methods of self-protection that have covered up these sinful areas in my life. Reveal what You are ready to heal. In Jesus' name. Amen.

TIPS FOR DAD

Try a 30-day experiment: for the numbered day of the month, read the corresponding chapter number of PSALMS and PROVERBS. For example, if today is the 16th, read PSALMS 16 and PROVERBS 16. PSALMS and PROVERBS are the "wisdom and praise" of God. It is so simple and easy to remember, but so profound. Even a short intimate time given to God daily will make significant change in your whole day...and eventually your whole life! It's a must for any godly man, husband, and father.

DAY 3

THE ANATOMY OF FLESH

BEGIN WITH PRAYER

Give God permission to shine His holy light into every "room" in your heart and ask His forgiveness where needed.

What happens when a rat dies in your attic and you don't discover it for several weeks? It stinks! There's nothing quite like the smell of rotting flesh. Or how about the smell of stinking flesh in the locker room after a game? Whew! That's like our flesh. When left alone, it causes a stink in our lives that smells up the place. It keeps us from being the husbands and fathers we want to be.

Scripture uses the Greek word *sarx*[2] for "flesh" in several ways. It can describe the earthly body (Gen. 2:21; Rom. 1:3), or all of mankind (Rom. 3:19-20), or *carnality* in Christians. That means people who have Christ within, but act as if He is not there. Today we'll look at this third use of "flesh."

Read Romans 7:15-25; 8:1-4 in your Bible.

Does the scenario described in these verses sound familiar? There is this battle between the flesh and Spirit in the life of a Christian.

Verse 16: *"But if I do the very thing I do not wish to do, I agree with the Law, confessing that it is good."*

I know when I'm doing wrong. It's clear from God's law written in Scripture and on my heart. The problem isn't in the law, it's in me.

Verse 17: *"So now, no longer am I the one doing it, but sin which indwells me."*

As a Christian, I'm a new creation. But since I'm still here on earth in a body that's capable of sin, sin is in me. Imagine sin as a tumor. A tumor may *affect* me, but it doesn't *define* me. The tumor isn't my identity. Likewise, identity and behavior are different. You are God's child. That is your identity. You may choose to behave in a sinful way, but that doesn't make you a dirty rotten sinner. It simply means you have fleshy, sinful areas that need cleansing and pruning.

Verses 18-19: *"For I know that nothing good dwells in me, that is, in my flesh; for the wishing is present in me, but the doing of the good is not. For the good that I wish, I do not do; but I practice the very evil that I do not wish."*

The problem is in my flesh or self-nature. My self-strength can't create fruit in God's kingdom. It may achieve things, but the end result has no eternal reward. Verse 19 is a snapshot of walking in the flesh. It's an internal war!

Verses 20-21: *"But if I am doing the very thing I do not wish, I am no longer the one doing it, but sin which dwells in me. I find then the principle that evil is present in me, the one who wishes to do good."*

Even though you want to be right, you struggle. Let me give you another picture.

Imagine being on a camping trip and having a raw, open wound on your leg. During the night, flies lay eggs in that wound, and soon flesh-eating maggots appear. You've got a problem! That raw wound might represent your flesh. It's an untreated, sick place in your life you have not yet surrendered to God. Maybe it's your eyes (is porn a problem?), or your mouth (do you yell, curse, or say demeaning, negative things to your family?), or your finances (gambling? credit problem?) are vulnerable areas. Satan like that fly, will make a bee line for your weakness and begin his attack. Sin is like those maggots. It starts with just a little indiscretion, but soon starts eating your life away.

VERSE 22: *"For I joyfully concur with the law of God in the inner man, but I see a different law in the members of my body, waging war against the law of my mind, and making me a prisoner of the law of sin which is in my members."*

24 *"What a wretched man I am! Who will rescue me from this body of death?* 25 *Thanks be to God—through Jesus Christ our Lord! So then, I myself in my mind am a slave to God's law, but in the sinful nature a slave to the law of sin..."*

ROMANS 8:1 *Therefore, there is now no condemnation for those who are in Christ Jesus,* 2 *because through Christ Jesus the law of the Spirit of life set me free from the law of sin and death.* 3 *For what the law was powerless to do in that it was weakened by the sinful nature, God did by sending his own Son in the likeness of sinful man to be a sin offering. And so he condemned sin in sinful man,* 4 *in order that the righteous requirements of the law might be fully met in us, who do not live according to the sinful nature but according to the Spirit.*

EUREKA! We are not forever trapped by the vicious cycle of sin-Satan-defeat. Victory lies in the new law of the Spirit of life in Christ Jesus. It sets you free from being trapped in a never-ending flesh war. And that's what the rest of our study is all about.

Lord, I want to be free from the law of sin and death and to live by the law of the Spirit of life in Christ Jesus. Only You can father my children perfectly. Only You can can set me free from my habitual sin. Please do it in me, through me, and for me. In Jesus' name I earnestly pray. Amen.

TIPS FOR DAD

Controlling flesh tends to make mountains out of molehills. Putting things in perspective as you go through your day will help. Whether it's a cranky boss, a spat with your wife, or a houseful of noisy kids—in reality, these are not life threatening situations. It's just part of normal daily life. If your children are fighting, you can lose your cool or remember that sibling rivalry is a part of raising a family. If you get caught in traffic, you can let your blood pressure get out of hand, or spend the extra time praying for those things you never find time to pray for. This week, surrender these situations to Christ's control.

DAY 4

THE NATURE OF FLESH

BEGIN WITH PRAYER

Ask God to peel away the layers of flesh that cover your mind and keep you from knowing the truth about yourself and about Him.

Flesh has several characteristics. Flesh is controlling, rejecting, and sometimes like an octopus. I want you to see some illustrations of flesh found in Scripture. You may get uncomfortable when you begin to see yourself, but if we are going to be free, we have to be honest with ourselves. One of the main characteristics of flesh is that it is *controlling*. Remember, flesh reaches out to control and pulls in to satisfy.

Jacob and Laban

Read Genesis 29:15-30 in your Bible.

Jacob met his match when he met up with Laban. Jacob's name means "supplanter" and he already had a reputation for being a shrewd businessman. Jacob was seeking a wife (verses 1-14) and felt like he had found the right one in Rachel.

Laban, his father-in-law, had a case of controlling flesh. Laban not only wanted Jacob to work for his daughter Rachel, he wanted a husband for his oldest daughter. So, according to the local custom, he manipulated and controlled Jacob, forcing him to marry Leah by trickery. If you read further in Genesis 31, you will see that Jacob wanted to run from Laban. In verse 6, Jacob sends word to Rachel and Leah, *"You know that I've worked for your father with all my strength, yet your father has cheated me by changing my wages ten times."* Laban was the ultimate controlling dad...and he ultimately lost his children and grandchildren because of it!

In what area are you tempted to exhibit controlling flesh? Do you see yourself? Don't despair, Dad. Walking in the Spirit instead of walking in the flesh is a process. You and I are not going to "get it" all on the first day...or week...or year. But you will be amazed one day to realize that you are becoming freer from flesh patterns and freer to walk with Jesus through this journey of being a godly father.

Lord Jesus, here I am. You have known about my flesh all along and You still love me. Lord, I am amazed at that great love. Now, in Your love, guide me into all truth, especially about myself. Thank You, Lord. In Jesus' precious name I pray this. Amen.

TIPS FOR DAD

Family mealtime is important. Make coming home for dinner a priority. Encourage the family to eat at home often. Your children (and wife) need to see your willingness to help as well as your leadership in making this a fun, sharing time.

DAY 5

WHEN "I GOTTA HAVE IT" GETS YOU

BEGIN WITH PRAYER

Ask God to destroy wrong thought patterns and to take every thought captive to the obedience of Christ.

It's ugly, but true: We're all caught up somehow in "keeping up with the Joneses." Why? Somehow we feel it will meet the needs of our hearts. Society usually rewards handsome, smart, rich people. It penalizes ugly, dumb, poor people. Christians are not immune. We want our kids to be accepted and to be on top. Sadly, we'll do almost anything to make it happen.

Read I Peter 2:11 and Romans 13:13-14 in your Bible.

In Scripture, lust is more than sexual craving. It's is a strong desire of any kind, a morbid appetite to enjoy or possess something forbidden. We men can all understand sexual lust. But any craving outside God's will is by definition, lust. Craving money, power, sex, or possessions outside God's will is lust. Heaping up money and possessions to make you feel accepted or secure is walking in the flesh. Stepping on others in your climb to obtain power is lust. And of course, visiting porn websites and downloading pornographic videos is feeding a lust that will destroy your marriage and your life. That addiction has killed many marriages both inside and outside the church.

Read Galatians 5:19-21 in your Bible.

We can't ignore the glaring sexual flesh and sin. Are you caught up in an adulterous affair? End it today, Dad, and go home to your family – physically *and* emotionally. Are you addicted to pornography? You can be forgiven, but you must repent. Ask God and your wife to forgive you and put this thing behind you. You can't be free until you do. If you're in either of these situations, call a Christian counselor, godly friend, or pastor for help. Jesus can cleanse, heal and forgive. Come to Him with this today.

Read James 1:13-15 and 4:1-8 in your Bible.

Lust baits us and reels us in like a fisherman with his catch. If we allow a lustful thought to be conceived in us, sin and destruction will be born out in us. The word *lust* used in James 4:2 is the word *epithumeo*. It means "to set the heart upon, i.e. long for; covet, desire, lust after."[3] Have you set your heart on something (other than Christ) to make you feel significant, powerful or secure? Is God shining His light on any area of lustful flesh in you? How can we be free from lustful flesh? You'll learn more later in this course, but for now let me leave you with this.

Read Galatians 5:13-15.

13 You, my brothers, were called to be free. But do not use your freedom to indulge the sinful nature; rather, serve one another in love. 14 The entire law is summed up in a single command: "Love your neighbor as yourself." 15 If you keep on biting and devouring each other, watch out or you will be destroyed by each other.

The first step is to love. Love the Lord your God with all your heart, your soul, your mind, and your body. And love your neighbor as yourself. If you love, you won't lust. It's a simple first step that will set your feet on the right path.

Stay with me as we continue this important look at ourselves. I know this is getting sticky, but we must look at ourselves honestly if we are ever going to be free. Don't feel like the lone ranger...I am convicted on every page. But I have discovered the more honest I am with God, the more I see Him bring healing and wholeness, transforming my thinking both as a husband and as a father. The pain is worth the price!

Lord, I am seeing myself in a new light. Continue to reveal the flesh in me. Cleanse and renew me day by day. In Jesus' name. Amen.

TIPS FOR DAD

How can we be men of purity in a sex-saturated world? First, we must be honest with God. Begin with a daily quiet time. Confess specific lustful thoughts from the past day or week. Tell God who, where, when the problem is. Pray II Corinthians 10:5. When met with temptation, pray this prayer of taking every thought captive to the obedience of Christ. Be practical: get an internet filter; skip that TV show or movie; don't stare into a woman's eyes unless she's your wife!

WEEKEND STUDY

A DAD'S ATTITUDE

If you have a domineering, controlling pattern of thought and behavior toward your children, and you sew a patch of God's Word onto your parenting from PROVERBS that instructs us to discipline our children, you might be too harsh and authoritarian. The domineering, controlling-to-get-your-needs-met patterns need to be transformed into new patterns of thought that comes from Jesus, who carefully disciplines us for the glory of God and for our good. Conversely, if you have passive, permissive, people-pleasing patterns of thought toward your children, and you fill that old wineskin with the new wine of God's Word from I JOHN that instructs us to love one another, you might be fearful of setting boundaries for your children and withhold Godly discipline from them.

Take a few moments to evaluate a few areas of your life as a husband and father, by taking the test below.

"DAD'S ATTITUDE CHECK" TEST:

Are you exercising self-gratification (pulling in to satisfy) or self-legislation (reaching out to control) in:

DISCIPLINING/NOT DISCIPLINING YOUR CHILD?

For example: Are you disciplining your child too harshly in an effort to protect your reputation? Are you over-controlling him so he won't embarrass you at church, at school or with your family and friends? Do you see how that can be a form of self-legislation? Are you trying to control him to satisfy your personal need for peace and quiet?

Or are you gratifying yourself by being overly permissive, allowing your child to disobey your directives, because you are too lazy to discipline? Is pleasing your child more important to you than his character development?

YOUR CHILD'S SCHOOL SITUATION?

For example: Are you attempting to control your child's coach or teacher? Have you gone beyond being concerned to being controlling?

YOUR WORK/RECREATION SCHEDULE?

For example: Is your work/play schedule designed to honor God, to minister to your wife and children and to build your home? Or is it causing you to go on a "flesh trip" of gratifying self to the exclusion of all others?

YOUR CHILD'S EATING/SLEEPING/EXERCISING HABITS?

For example: Is your child's schedule set to meet your personal needs or is it set because it is what is best for that child and the whole family? Are you permissive with your child to get your need for acceptance met? Are you not willing to pay the price to discipline your children?

Now read GALATIANS 6:8-10 and apply these truth of these verses to your family.

"CONTROLLING" VERSUS DISCIPLINING OUR CHILDREN

As fathers, we are tempted to be controlling in many ways. We might use hostile behavior. We yell and scream to frighten our kids into doing what we want. Sometimes we use blackmail. "If you don't do what I say, I'll...." Sometimes we have a critical attitude and attack them personally. "You have never gotten that right!" We might be tempted to use guilt to control our children. "I paid so much money to get that for you and look what you've done."

Often we misuse body language to get in control. We stamp our feet or slam our hands on the table. We might even resort to the silent treatment, blocking out our wife or our children. This is not being a good father. These are fleshy attempts at being in control instead of using our God-given authority to lead our families. But you might be thinking, "Aren't dads supposed to be in control?

Parents are to take authority over their children (EPHESIANS 6:1). We are to assume the position of responsibility for the training and rearing of the child. EPHESIANS 6:4 says, "Fathers, do not provoke your children to anger, but bring them up in the discipline and instruction of the Lord." Yelling and all the other methods of controlling our children in the flesh reduce our position of authority. It says, "I'm trying to be in control here but I don't want to do what it really takes to discipline you—I'm too lazy to spend quality time training you. I want control you because it meets my needs!"

There is a better way. We should set a standard of behavior for our children not because it meets our needs, but because it is in the best interest of the child. Our children need the standard set in a firm but calm manner. "Susan, look at my eyes. You may not jump on the bed." "David, listen to my voice. You must come to me the first time I call you." "Jennifer, your curfew is 10:30. It is not 10:40. You must be inside the house at 10:30 according to the digital clock in the kitchen. Are we absolutely clear on that?" Then if they do not obey, don't yell at them or use manipulation and guilt to make them obey. Take action.

If your child deliberately, defiantly disobeys in rebellion against your authority, it is time for discipline. If your child is between the ages of 2 and 12, it may be time for a spanking. The Bible instructs us in the book of Proverbs to discipline with a rod.

Read the following verses from PROVERBS, noting the form of discipline in each verse:

PROVERBS 10:13 PROVERBS 13:24 PROVERBS 29:15
PROVERBS 20:30 PROVERBS 22:15
PROVERBS 23:14 PROVERBS 26:3

Yelling is unnecessary. The reason we raise our voice is because we are unwilling to take the appropriate action. I am convinced that those who oppose spanking and other forms of discipline see it as just a means of adults exerting fleshly "control" over defenseless children. And in some cases, they would be correct.

But Biblical "chastisement" or spanking with a rod done "in the spirit" is a means of teaching our children to submit to authority. A proper spanking is done on the buttocks with 2 or 3 firm swats with a rod or paddle that sting but do not bruise. We don't spank on the legs and we never degrade our children by hitting, slapping or popping them on the face.

Spanking needs to be reserved for deliberate, defiant, direct disobedience. Other means of discipline—such as withholding privileges—should be used for childish irresponsibility. Pre-schoolers are in an intense training phase. They are not little adults. Teaching an expected behavior will take months of consistent training. Monitor and adjust your discipline according to your child. It is possible to "over-spank" and to "under-spank." This is why you need to stay on your knees praying for God's guidance and listen to godly wisdom from your wife and mentors.

If you have a teenager who rebels against your authority, remove the privileges that come with responsible behavior. Most teens want to drive a car (that you bought), go out with friends, listen to the jam box (that you bought) and/or talk on the phone (that you pay for). Calmly remove the privileges that come with living in your house under your house rules. Don't respond to their emotional outbursts with your own. You can take authority over your teen without resorting to walking in the flesh (but it will require a great deal of prayer!).

Sit down in the living room or at the dining room table with your pre-teen or teenager and outline your standards for their behavior. Set curfews, dress codes, homework rules, church attendance requirements, work and chore expectations and whatever else is important to you. Then if they choose to disobey, resist the urge to control them in the flesh. You'll be tempted to yell at them. However, you can calmly but with absolute unwavering authority take action.

The ultimate authority to which we are leading them to submit their lives is the authority of God. If they will not submit to your authority, they will not submit to God's. If you discipline selfishly—too hard or too soft—to meet your desire to get what you want, when you want it, the way you want it, your child will suffer.

Our kids have radar about that sort of thing. They know when we are operating in the flesh. But if you discipline your children with a pure heart desiring to lead them to submit to the authority of God, it will bear fruit in the lives of your children.

Notes

[1] *Heart's Cry,* Jennifer Kennedy Dean, New Hope Publishing, Birmingham, Alabama, *p. 15.*

[2] *The New Strong's Exhaustive Concordance of the Bible, Greek Dictionary of the New Testament,* James Strong, LL.D., S.T.D., Thomas Nelson Publishers, 4561, p. 64.

[3] Ibid., Number 1937, p. 31

WEEK 3

THE PRINCIPLE OF THE BRANCH: COMMON TRAPS FOR DADS

Which traps do you fall into most as a father? Most of us know exactly how our parents failed us, but we don't like to spend time thinking about our own weaknesses that are causing our families grief. You might have said, "When I have a family, I'll never treat them like my dad treated me, but somehow, you hear the same words coming from your mouth. How can we change this pattern from passing along to our own kids and then to their children? How can we grow, learn, and change? First, we have to be courageous and take the time to look within...

FatherWise Group Prayer Requests

The first person in the group will share a one sentence prayer request about his wife or his children. Each person in the group will pray a one sentence prayer over that request before moving on to the next person's request. The group will continue in this way until everyone has prayed over each request.

DAY 1

PRIDEFUL, "KNOW IT ALL" FLESH

BEGIN WITH PRAYER

Ask our Heavenly Father to sweep clean every corner of your heart and purify you according to His will.

COLOSSIANS 2:18-19 tells us that anyone who delights in false humility or is puffed up has *"lost connection with the Head [Christ]."* I JOHN 2:16 says that *"For all that is in the world, the lust of the flesh and the lust of the eyes and the boastful pride of life, is not from the Father, but is from the world."*

When a man is prideful, it is particularly debilitating for his family.

This variety of flesh can keep you from seeking the mentoring and teaching you need to become a good husband and father from other men. It can keep you from listening to your wife when she's trying to tell you the truth. It can make you stubborn and unapproachable to your children. The jokes about men not wanting to ask directions or get help aren't so funny! When we become a "know-it-all" who is never wrong, our families find it impossible to communicate with us. When communication breaks down, the family's in trouble.

For me, one of the hardest experiences with prideful flesh occurred in a work situation. One of the men working for me had a lot of knowledge about our project, but his prideful attitude made him incredibly difficult to work with. I had to treat him very delicately when I needed to point out areas where he needed to improve some of his work that wasn't acceptable. I wonder how his wife and children enjoy living with a man like this...someone who can never be wrong.

PROVERBS 16:18 says, *"Pride goes before destruction, a haughty spirit before a fall."*

The Hebrew word for pride in is *ga'own*. It means "arrogancy, excellency, majesty, pomp, pride, proud, swelling."[1] When I approach fatherhood with pride or *ga'own* (that even *sounds* bad), I am going to fail.

Have your children ever embarrassed you? Does your little "pride and joy" have egg on his face sometimes? When you are embarrassed over your children's behavior or performance, stop a moment and ask the Lord, "Am I prideful? Do I really just want my kids to make me look good? Is this my flesh problem, not necessarily theirs?"

What is God bringing to your mind concerning prideful flesh?

I know you are probably ready to move on to a new subject, but we need to dig a little deeper. We're going to be courageous and ask Jesus to keep on working in our hearts. No one ever called heart-surgery a picnic. But this is the way to freedom, so roll up your sleeves and let's continue.

Lord, don't stop working in my heart even when it is painful. Cleanse me and purge me from destructive patterns in my life that affect me and everyone around me, especially my wife and children. I am turning toward You, Lord, and I will not flinch as You prune my life. I pray that You will continue the good work You have begun in me. I pray this in the name of the Lord Jesus who loves me. Amen.

TIPS FOR DAD

In the area of pride, one of the hardest things as a dad is to admit wrong or have your children see you make a mistake. Dad, we must be honest with our kids... sometimes we ARE wrong, and we DO make mistakes! If you will admit it, this will endear your children to you and help them identify with you. Ask your children to pray for you as a father, sharing with them your struggles and joys. I don't mean "airing out your laundry" but being honest enough to share your heart's desire to be a godly father.

DAY 2

PASSIVE, "MILQUETOAST" FLESH

BEGIN WITH PRAYER

Ask God to shine His light in every corner of your heart. Remember, this is not a time of morbid introspection. Let the Lord "search your heart...and lead you in the way everlasting" (PSALM 139:23-24).

Perhaps you have a mild-mannered personality. Everyone likes you because you are easy to be around. You don't rock the boat. You are gentle and kind and probably have the spiritual gift of mercy. Dad, that's great when dealing with adults, but it could ruin the lives of your children if you don't know how to set appropriate boundaries with them and make those boundaries stick.

Most parents we encounter who have this type of personality have a child of the opposite personality. They usually have a bull-headed little tyrant who orders them around from the delivery room! Why does God assign these parents and children to one another? Can't you guess? They become the "iron that sharpens iron." They bring balance into each other's lives. They need each other to reveal and chisel away at the flesh.

The Bible gives us insight into one Dad with passive flesh patterns in regard to his children.

I SAMUEL 2:12-25

12 Eli's sons were wicked men; they had no regard for the LORD.

13 Now it was the practice of the priests with the people that whenever anyone offered a sacrifice and while the meat was being boiled, the servant of the priest would come with a three-pronged fork in his hand. 14 He would plunge it into the pan or kettle or caldron or pot, and the priest would take for himself whatever the fork brought up. This is how they treated all the Israelites who came to Shiloh. 15 But even before the fat was burned, the servant of the priest would come and say to the man who was sacrificing, "Give the priest some meat to roast; he won't accept boiled meat from you, but only raw."

16 If the man said to him, "Let the fat be burned up first, and then take whatever you want," the servant would then answer, "No, hand it over now; if you don't, I'll take it by force."

17 This sin of the young men was very great in the LORD's sight, for they were treating the LORD's offering with contempt.

18 But Samuel was ministering before the LORD -a boy wearing a linen ephod. 19 Each year his mother made him a little robe and took it to him when she went up with her husband to offer the annual sacrifice. 20 Eli would bless Elkanah and his wife, saying, "May the LORD give you children by this woman to take the place of the one she prayed for and gave to the LORD." Then they would go home. 21 And the LORD was gracious to Hannah; she conceived and gave birth to three sons and two daughters. Meanwhile, the boy Samuel grew up in the presence of the LORD.

22 Now Eli, who was very old, heard about everything his sons were doing to all Israel and how they slept with the women who served at the entrance to the Tent of Meeting. 23 So he said to them, "Why do you do such things? I hear from all the people about these wicked deeds of yours. 24 No, my sons; it is not a good report that I hear spreading among the LORD's people. 25 If a man sins against another man, God may mediate for him; but if a man sins against the LORD, who will intercede for him?" His sons, however, did not listen to their father's rebuke...

Knowing that Eli was a priest, do you see something unusual about his sons? Don't you think it's odd that Eli was a priest and yet his sons did not know the Lord? Eli's sons were hoodlums! They were in the direct line of the priesthood, but they made a mockery of the priesthood.

Let's take a look at some of Eli's parenting practices. Was there anything he could have done differently? When his sons disobeyed the Lord, what did he do? What action did he take? He didn't take any action—he just spoke to them but they didn't listen to their father's rebuke. Had they learned to ignore their father's voice as young children? Had he ever trained them to hear his voice and obey?

Eli was held accountable for his sons because he honored his sons above the Lord. Eli "worshipped" his boys. He would not cross them. He would not set boundaries for their behavior and make them stick. He had passive parenting flesh. And he paid for it.

I SAMUEL 3:10-13

10The LORD came and stood there, calling as at the other times, "Samuel! Samuel!" Then Samuel said, "Speak, for your servant is listening."

11 And the LORD said to Samuel: "See, I am about to do something in Israel that will make the ears of everyone who hears of it tingle. 12 At that time I will carry out against Eli everything I spoke against his family—from beginning to end. 13 For I told him that I would judge his family forever because of the sin he knew about; his sons made themselves contemptible, <u>and he failed to restrain them</u>.

This story has a strong message. It strikes at the heart of every parent. Ask the Lord to show you if you are honoring your children above Him. Be still and allow God to do business in your life.

If you had a domineering mom or dad and you learned to be passive to stay out of their way, you'll probably struggle to be the spiritual head of your home. Leading your wife and kids won't come naturally. You'll need to spend time in prayer asking for the gift of godly authority. Begin taking steps of leadership by assessing your family's greatest need—is it better communication? Better time management? Obedience training for your younger children? More structure or less structure? Fewer outside-the-family commitments? Begin there with giving leadership and direction.

I want to share my story with you. As a parent of more than 30 years, this has been one of my weakest areas of parenting. My tendency is to lay back and not take the strong leadership needed in my home because I don't want to "rock the boat." As a man called to be the spiritual leader of his home, this can be disastrous.

I was tempted to make our kids my friends instead of being a parent. I wanted them to like me and think I was "cool." I was guilty of not taking a firm stand when I asked them to do something, and then I griped at them when they didn't do it! It was a no win situation for them. As a result I saw my children waver in the respect for authority. I blamed myself for it.

Now let me clarify this story somewhat. You see God had been at work in the flesh area of my life long before I was a father. As a husband, He began showing me my lack of leadership by being passive with Denise. The process He was taking me through in this area was only intensified when the role of parenting began to heat up. God began to clearly reveal my sins of passivity and that I was helpless to do anything about it in my own strength.

Only as I allow Jesus to "husband and parent" through me, do I see fruit in the lives of my wife and children. As I confessed this to my children and asked their prayerful support, God began to change their hearts as well. They have suffered from the consequences of my early sins, but as the years have passed, God in His mercy has blessed them and me with a new and more complete understanding of respect for authority.

Lord, forgive me for honoring my child above You. Forgive my passive patterns of behavior regarding my child and family. Lord, I need complete re-tooling as a parent. I am going to trust You to undertake that work for me and in me. In Jesus' name. Amen

TIPS FOR DAD

Every dad wants their child to be the best. But what is our motive? Often we push our kids toward good things for the wrong reasons, like boosting our own egos. It's easy to get caught up in performance-based acceptance. We need to take our cue from our Heavenly Father, who loves unconditionally, regardless of performance (Romans 8:38-39). We've been called to challenge our children to reach their highest calling in the kingdom. But that challenge must be couched in the same unconditional love and acceptance the Father shows us.

DAY 3

PIOUS, "BETTER THAN YOU" FLESH

BEGIN WITH PRAYER

Pray part of Psalm 139 back to God as a prayer.

1 O LORD, you have searched me and you know me.

2 You know when I sit and when I rise; you perceive my thoughts from afar.

3 You discern my going out and my lying down; you are familiar with all my ways.

4 Before a word is on my tongue you know it completely, O LORD.

5 You hem me in—behind and before; you have laid your hand upon me.

6 Such knowledge is too wonderful for me, too lofty for me to attain.

7 Where can I go from your Spirit? Where can I flee from your presence?

8 If I go up to the heavens, you are there; if I make my bed in the depths, you are there.

9 If I rise on the wings of the dawn, if I settle on the far side of the sea,

10 even there your hand will guide me, your right hand will hold me fast.

Today we're going to address "religious" flesh. Religious flesh gets its kicks out of being "righteous"—doing things for God to make us feel better and look better to other people. True righteousness glorifies God. Self-righteousness glorifies me. True righteousness makes God look good. Self-righteousness makes me look good.

Read MATTHEW 6:1-18.

1 Be careful not to do your "acts of righteousness" before men, to be seen by them. If you do, you will have no reward from your Father in heaven.

In the Sermon on the Mount, Jesus gave His disciples instruction in walking in the Spirit instead of in the flesh. He exposed common flesh patterns and taught what kingdom living looks like. Giving, praying and fasting should be done in secret. Why? Because we can get caught up in man's praise, even in the act of praising God!

"Religious" flesh expresses itself different ways. My religious flesh tends to express itself when I am at work around "ungodly" people. I sometimes feel uncomfortable around them and catch myself avoiding getting to know them. Perhaps you like to teach or preach or you're a deacon or elder of your church and you enjoy the status that comes with the territory.

PHILIPPIANS 2:3 says, *"Do nothing from selfishness or empty conceit..."* (NASB). Those words are translated "strife or vainglory" in the King James Version. The word for *vainglory* in Greek is *kenodoxia* and means "empty glorying or self-conceit."[2] What a picture of fruitless glorying in ourselves!

Our kids are especially allergic to religious flesh. They can see straight through us when we teach or preach one thing and act like another.

Matthew 23:1-12

1 Then Jesus said to the crowds and to his disciples: 2 "The teachers of the law and the Pharisees sit in Moses' seat. 3 So you must obey them and do everything they tell you. But do not do what they do, for they do not practice what they preach. 4 They tie up heavy loads and put them on men's shoulders, but they themselves are not willing to lift a finger to move them."

5 "Everything they do is done for men to see: They make their phylacteries wide and the tassels on their garments long; 6 they love the place of honor at banquets and the most important seats in the synagogues; 7 they love to be greeted in the marketplaces and to have men call them 'Rabbi.'

8 "But you are not to be called 'Rabbi,' for you have only one Master and you are all brothers. 9 And do not call anyone on earth 'father,' for you have one Father, and he is in heaven. 10 Nor are you to be called 'teacher,' for you have one Teacher, the Christ. 11 The greatest among you will be your servant. 12 For whoever exalts himself will be humbled, and whoever humbles himself will be exalted."

The Lord won't let us get by with outward religious rituals; He is interested in our hearts. When we come to Him in humility, worshipping Him in Spirit and in truth, it glorifies our Father and leads our children where we want them to go. Right into the presence of Jesus.

Lord, I want to be free of religious, pious flesh. I want to worship You in Spirit and in truth. Teach me how to worship, give and pray in secret. I give You all the glory and honor. In Jesus' name. Amen.

TIPS FOR DAD

Pray for and with your children before bedtime. Even toddlers can sense your heart. Praying with your child tells him he's important to you and builds a unique spirit-oneness with him. And don't let that teenager stop you. He may seem uninterested, but it's exactly what he needs.

DAY 4

PITIFUL, "QUARRELSOME" FLESH

BEGIN WITH PRAYER

Begin with prayer. Praise the Lord for all the blessings He has given you and your family. Ask Him to prepare your heart for His Word.

You may have grown up in a home where fighting and arguing was a way of life. Your parents may have screamed or physically abused each other. Maybe they abused you. Perhaps your father yelled as his only form of discipline. Now, you may find yourself using the same ineffective means to discipline your children.

Recognizing the hurtful ways of the past is the first step to becoming free from them. Then you need to forgive those who have hurt you—physically, verbally or emotionally. If there was abuse, seek professional help from a godly, Christian counselor to help you process the grief and to get on the other side of it to freedom.

Maybe your case is not that extreme. Maybe you're just a quarrelsome kind of guy who likes to get his way.

Read I Corinthians 3:1-3.

Brothers, I could not address you as spiritual but as worldly—mere infants in Christ. I gave you milk, not solid food, for you were not yet ready for it. Indeed, you are still not ready. You are still worldly. For since there is jealousy and quarreling among you, are you not worldly? Are you not acting like mere men?

Based on the evidence of their jealous and quarrelsome behavior, Paul calls the Corinthians unspiritual and "mere infants." Likewise, the disciples quarreled at the Lord's supper.

Read the account in LUKE 22:14-24.

14 When the hour came, Jesus and his apostles reclined at the table. 15
And he said to them, "I have eagerly desired to eat this Passover with
you before I suffer. 16 For I tell you, I will not eat it again until it finds
fulfillment in the kingdom of God."

17 After taking the cup, he gave thanks and said, "Take this and divide
it among you. 18 For I tell you I will not drink again of the fruit of the
vine until the kingdom of God comes."

19 And he took bread, gave thanks and broke it, and gave it to them,
saying, "This is my body given for you; do this in remembrance of me."

20 In the same way, after the supper he took the cup, saying, "This cup
is the new covenant in my blood, which is poured out for you. 21 But
the hand of him who is going to betray me is with mine on the table.

22 The Son of Man will go as it has been decreed, but woe to that man who betrays him." 23 They began to question among themselves which of them it might be who would do this.

24 Also a dispute arose among them as to which of them was considered to be greatest.

Jesus had just told the disciples that one of them would betray Him, and they began to discuss which one it would be. Then suddenly, the topic changed to who of them was the greatest! Can you see the "flesh trip" they were on?

In what relationship might a man might be tempted to be quarrelsome and act like a baby? And what price will you pay if you walk in the flesh in this relationship?

Read I Peter 3:7.

Husbands, in the same way be considerate as you live with your wives, and treat them with respect as the weaker partner and as heirs with you of the gracious gift of life, so that nothing will hinder your prayers.

If you choose to be inconsiderate and childish in your marriage, even your prayers can be "hindered." That's not good! Quarrelsome, infantile behavior with your wife is the *opposite* of walking in the Spirit as her spiritual leader. In fact, James 3:13-16 tells us:

Who is wise and understanding among you? Let him show it by his good life, by deeds done in the humility that comes from wisdom. But if you harbor bitter envy and selfish ambition in your hearts, do not boast about it or deny the truth. Such "wisdom" does not come down from heaven but is earthly, unspiritual, of the devil. For where you have envy and selfish ambition, there you find disorder and every evil practice.

Read Proverbs 10:19 and 20:3.

19 When words are many, sin is not absent, but he who holds his tongue is wise.

3 It is to a man's honor to avoid strife, but every fool is quick to quarrel.

Shooting from the hip and shooting off the lip is never a good way to relate to your wife. A wise husband carefully chooses his words. It's foolish to pick fights with your wife or kids. Ephesians 6:4 instructs, *"Fathers, do not provoke your children to anger, but bring them up in the discipline and instruction of the Lord."* Has there been an incident lately where you have provoked your child to anger?

Then it's time to take an honest look at your present circumstance. Is the Holy Spirit convicting you of your own behavioral problems as a father? If so, come to Him. Confess your sins. Ask for His cleansing and pruning so you can be free to love and discipline your children in His Spirit. Then go to your wife and children and ask their forgiveness. You'll be amazed at the changes He can bring about in your home!

Lord, I'm beginning to see things from Your point of view. Enable me to look honestly at my past and my present behaviors. Heal, cleanse and lead me. I pray this in Jesus' name. Amen.

TIPS FOR DAD

I see much of myself in my children, and some of it is flesh. The Bible teaches that the "sins of the father" can be carried to the third and fourth generation. As God reveals the flesh areas of your life that you're beginning to see in your child, ask Him to stop the generational curse right now! Seek His wisdom in sharing this prayer request with your child at an appropriate time when he will understand the significance of this prayer. God wants you and your children free!

DAY 5

PERSISTENTLY SELF-CENTERED "I, ME, MINE" FLESH

BEGIN WITH PRAYER

Offer your heart to God as a living sacrifice. Ask Him to take it, melt it and mold it according to His perfect will. Let God do all that He wants to do in your life today.

This is our last day to study the flesh. Aren't you glad? I don't think we could have stood it for one more day! But cleaning out the old is the way to prepare for the new patterns of thinking and new actions we'll be working on in the following weeks.

You can't be an effective father and be centered on yourself at the same time. The name of the game in fathering is self-sacrifice. I'll be the first to concede that dads need recreation, and there is a place for "time out" from our children. But the principle here is giving up the right to be "priority one"—getting your needs met ahead of your wife and children.

PHILIPPIANS 2:3-4.

Do nothing out of selfish ambition or vain conceit, but in humility consider others better than yourselves. Each of you should look not only to your own interests, but also to the interests of others.

In reality, all flesh is self-centered. Being self-centered and self-absorbed has become a global pastime. We're told to "take time for ourselves" and "look out for number one, because no one else will." No one else will because *they're* so self-absorbed! Is this how we're to live?

What destruction we have caused in our homes from self-centeredness! What devastation reigns because we are a people who are self-absorbed!

The antidote for self-serving flesh—in fact, for all flesh—is found in the rest of the passage in Philippians.

Read PHILIPPIANS 2:5-11.

> 5 *Your attitude should be the same as that of Christ Jesus:*
>
> 6 *Who, being in very nature God, did not consider equality with God something to be grasped,*
>
> 7 *but made himself nothing, taking the very nature of a servant, being made in human likeness.*
>
> 8 *And being found in appearance as a man, he humbled himself and became obedient to death—even death on a cross!*
>
> 9 *Therefore God exalted him to the highest place and gave him the name that is above every name,*

10 that at the name of Jesus every knee should bow, in heaven and on earth and under the earth,
11 and every tongue confess that Jesus Christ is Lord, to the glory of God the Father.

We must take our cue from Christ Jesus. What did Jesus do to avoid self-serving flesh? What price did He pay to completely humble Himself? Jesus emptied Himself and humbled Himself to the point of death—death on the Cross. That what it takes to get rid of self-centered flesh.

Don't miss next week, because we will finally find the way to freedom from all this flesh!

Lord, please cleanse me of my self-centeredness. Love my wife and children through me unselfishly, I pray. In Jesus' name. Amen.

TIPS FOR DAD

One of the best ways for you to be a great father is in being a great husband to your wife. Children will obey and respect Mom more completely when they see the genuine love, attention, and praise given to her from Dad. Here are a few ways to show the kids you really love your wife:

1. Take your wife on dates...regularly. Leave the kids with the grandparents or babysitter. Plan it out and make it fun. You will both be better parents if you give yourselves a regular break from the kids.
2. Brag on your wife in front of your children. I know, this is a hard one... it was for me, but you can do it! Try praying praise for your wife (PROVERBS 31) in your quiet time. This will make it much easier!
3. Don't be afraid to show affection to your wife in front of the kids... just don't get carried away. Children need to see the love their parents have for each other.

WEEKEND STUDY

OTHER MEN IN THE BIBLE

Let's examine the flesh patterns of two other men in the Bible.

Read JUDGES 6:11-27.

11 The angel of the LORD came and sat down under the oak in Ophrah that belonged to Joash the Abiezrite, where his son Gideon was threshing wheat in a winepress to keep it from the Midianites.
12 When the angel of the LORD appeared to Gideon, he said, "The LORD is with you, mighty warrior."

13 "But sir," Gideon replied, "if the LORD is with us, why has all this happened to us? Where are all his wonders that our fathers told us about when they said, 'Did not the LORD bring us up out of Egypt?' But now the LORD has abandoned us and put us into the hand of Midian."

14 The LORD turned to him and said, "Go in the strength you have and save Israel out of Midian's hand. Am I not sending you?"

15 "But Lord , " Gideon asked, "how can I save Israel? My clan is the weakest in Manasseh, and I am the least in my family."

16 The LORD answered, "I will be with you, and you will strike down all the Midianites together."

17 Gideon replied, "If now I have found favor in your eyes, give me a sign that it is really you talking to me. 18 Please do not go away until I
come back and bring my offering and set it before you." And the LORD said, "I will wait until you return."

19 Gideon went in, prepared a young goat, and from an ephah of flour he made bread without yeast. Putting the meat in a basket and its broth in a pot, he brought them out and offered them to him under the oak.

*20 The angel of God said to him, "Take the meat and the unleavened
bread, place them on this rock, and pour out the broth." And Gideon
did so. 21 With the tip of the staff that was in his hand, the angel of
the LORD touched the meat and the unleavened bread. Fire flared
from the rock, consuming the meat and the bread. And the angel of the
LORD disappeared. 22 When Gideon realized that it was the angel
of the LORD, he exclaimed, "Ah, Sovereign LORD! I have seen the
angel of the LORD face to face!"*

*23 But the LORD said to him, "Peace! Do not be afraid. You are not
going to die."*

*24 So Gideon built an altar to the LORD there and called it The
LORD is Peace. To this day it stands in Ophrah of the Abiezrites.*

*25 That same night the LORD said to him, "Take the second bull from
your father's herd, the one seven years old. Tear down your father's
altar to Baal and cut down the Asherah pole beside it. 26 Then build
a proper kind of altar to the LORD your God on the top of this height.
Using the wood of the Asherah pole that you cut down, offer the second
bull as a burnt offering."*

*27 So Gideon took ten of his servants and did as the LORD told him.
But because he was afraid of his family and the men of the town, he did
it at night rather than in the daytime.*

(If you're not familiar with the story of Gideon, read all of JUDGES 6). The story of Gideon is a prime example of passive flesh. Gideon just didn't want to rock the boat. He was paralyzed by fear. It was easy for anyone to bully him. When God found him, he was beating out wheat in a winepress instead of out in the open so he could hide from his enemies. At the end of our passage, he was obeying God under cover of night because he was afraid of his own relatives and the men of his hometown!

Do you find yourself hiding from responsibilities? Are you trapped in fearful thinking patterns? As you think through this, ask God to give you courage and faith in each area where you've been fearful.

Let's look at a Biblical account of another parent who exhibited passive flesh. Skim read several chapters in II Samuel 13 and 15-18 to get the full story sequence.

David, the man after God's own heart, often operated in the flesh when it came to his children. David was a passive father, getting angry, but doing nothing about the gross sins of his children. David just refused to deal with the problems, and the problems in his family didn't go away. They escalated. And destruction came to his children.

You want to be a good dad, or you wouldn't be in this course. I want to say I'm proud of you for coming and for doing the study in Scripture. You don't have to be defeated by your past or trapped in your current ways of doing things at home. You can change by the miraculous power of Jesus Christ. He WILL set you free from every area you bring to Him for healing and transformation. You won't be the same man after encountering Jesus. He is the one—and the only one—who can make these changes. So come to Him. Be honest and lay it all out before Him. Let Him work and when He does, you'll be a new man.

Lord, thank You for the children You've given me. They are truly a blessing from You. Please continue to chisel away the flesh in my life for the sake of my children, Lord. Forgive me for my negative patterns of behavior regarding them. Hear my prayer for them and for me. In Jesus' name. Amen.

Notes

[1] *Strong's Hebrew and Chaldee Dictionary,* (Nashville, Tenn.: Thomas Nelson Publishers, 1984) Number 1347, 25.

[2] *Strong's Greek Dictionary,* (Nashville, Tenn.: Thomas Nelson Publishers, 1984) Number 2754, 41.

WEEK 4

THE PRINCIPLE OF THE SHEARS: PRUNING THE BRANCH

Now we've discovered the problem. We're sometimes full of ourselves and don't have room to be filled with God. So how do we get rid of the problem? Take a few more self-help seminars? Pull ourselves up by our boot straps? No. The answer is found at the foot of the cross.

FatherWise Group Prayer Requests

The first person in the group will share a one sentence prayer request about his wife or his children. Each person in the group will pray a one sentence prayer over that request before moving on to the next person's request. The group will continue in this way until everyone has prayed over each request.

DAY 1

THE PRINCIPLE OF THE CROSS

BEGIN WITH PRAYER

Ask the Father to remove any barrier keeping you from Him. Ask Him to accomplish His purpose in your life.

JOHN 15:1-2.

1 "I am the true vine, and my Father is the gardener. 2 He cuts off every branch in me that bears no fruit, while every branch that does bear fruit he prunes so that it will be even more fruitful."

God prunes branches that bear fruit. You may say, "Wait a minute, you mean if I'm a believer, and I'm bearing the fruit of love, joy, peace, patience, etc., He will come into my life with the pruning shears and start cutting? Why would He do that?" What does the verse say? He prunes so you will bear MORE fruit. If we truly want to bear more fruit, to live lives that are pouring forth love and joy and peace, then we'll need to submit to the Heavenly pruning shears. We must allow Him to cut away that which keeps us from bearing more fruit.

We discovered in the last two sections what needs to be cut away: flesh. Let's review what "flesh" looks like.

Flesh, or self-nature, is like an octopus. We could label the arms *jealousy, hate, anger, fear, pride, lust, envy,* and *unforgiveness*. The arms of your "flesh" octopus might include *gluttony, greed* and others.

Read GALATIANS 5:16-21, making note of the "deeds of the flesh" listed in these verses. What titles would the arms of your "flesh" octopus have?

What happens when you cut off the arms of an octopus? They grow back! If you want to permanently get rid of the arm of an octopus, there is only one thing to do. You must kill the octopus. There must be a mortal wound to the head.

We know that "flesh" often rears its ugly head even in devout believers. But there is a cure.

ROMANS 8:1-4.

1 Therefore, there is now no condemnation for those who are in Christ Jesus, 2 because through Christ Jesus the law of the Spirit of life set me free from the law of sin and death. 3 For what the law was powerless to do in that it was weakened by the sinful nature, God did by sending his own Son in the likeness of sinful man to be a sin offering. And so he condemned sin in sinful man, 4 in order that the righteous requirements of the law might be fully met in us, who do not live according to the sinful nature but according to the Spirit.

LAW OF SIN AND DEATH VS. LAW OF THE SPIRIT OF LIFE IN CHRIST

The Old Testament or Old Covenant stated that when you sin, you will die (DEUTERONOMY 30:15-20). That is called the Law of Sin and Death. When you live out the attitudes and actions of your fleshy self-nature, you are living according to the Law of Sin and Death. If you indulge yourself in lustful behavior, your body will be put on a path of destruction. If you are unforgiving of some offense against you, your mind and spirit are cut off from the life-flow of Jesus, and you will experience deadness. (This doesn't mean you

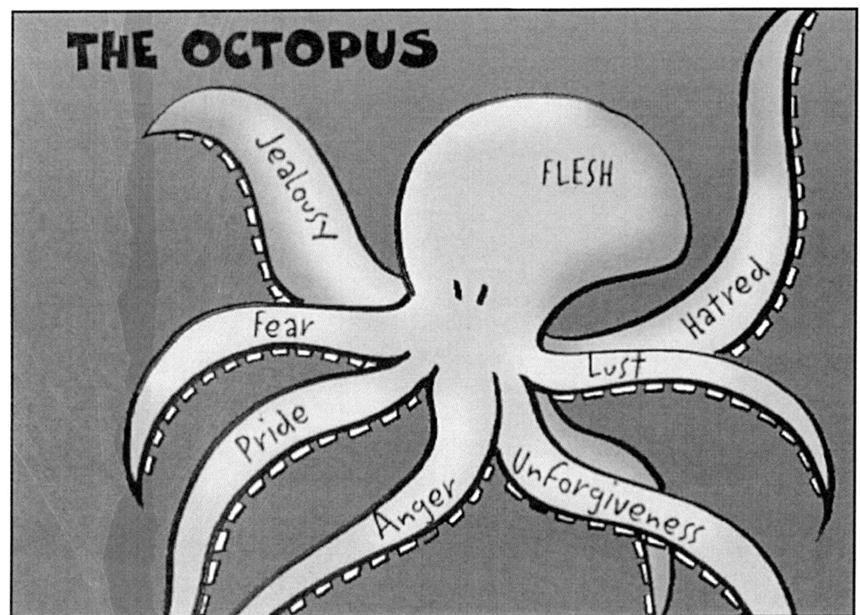

are no longer a Christian, but that your fellowship with Him is disrupted.) When Jesus died on the cross, He set us free from that Law of Sin and Death.

Here's how He did it. He became sin, and so He died. That was the legal payment for becoming a sinner. So He fulfilled the Law of Sin.

But then, because He is God of the Universe who is all powerful, He victoriously rose from the dead in full resurrection power and came to life again. That's how He set us free from the Law of Death. His death paid the penalty of sin, and His resurrection life set us free to live. We are no longer trapped into a sin and death cycle.

Do you hear that, Dad? You are free! If you've accepted His death in place of yours as payment for your sins, you're truly free! You're free to live according to the Law of the Spirit of Life in Christ Jesus instead of the Law of Sin and Death.

What does all that mean for a father who is overworked and underpaid, with a bunch of kids who whine, teenagers who talk back or adult children who never come home for a visit, or even worse, young adults who've moved back home? It means that if we are in Christ, we do not have to be trapped by our self-nature or "flesh" into destructive patterns of thinking and responding to those trying parenting situations.

We don't have to lash out at whiny children, or condemn ourselves for poor job performance, or despair over young adults who are drifting. We don't have to be constantly defeated by our own behavior or the behavior of our kids. We aren't bound to the Law of Sin and Death.

Let me give you another example. Let's say you come from a long line of men who yell at their children to get them under control. Your granddad may have yelled at your dad, and your dad yelled at you. So when you had children, it was "natural" to yell at them whenever you wanted to get them to obey you.

So can that cycle be broken? Can you stop yelling and start giving firm, but kind commands to children who will obey the first time they hear your calm voice? Is that a dream? Would you like to be free?

Freedom for Fathers

Jesus died on the cross and rose again just so we could be free in situations like that. Sometimes we think He died and rose again just so we could go to heaven. Of course, He did, but there is so much more to it than that! He died and rose again so you could live in freedom here on this earth in very earthy situations like yelling or not yelling at kids. The cross of Jesus is very, very practical. If you understand it, it will change your daily routine. It will affect every moment of your life. You will never be the same.

Yes, Dad. You can be free from yelling or any other fleshy response you have with your children and your wife. There is a way out of that defeating cycle of sin and death in your relationships. It is the way of the cross.

The cross is the pruning shear in God's hand. But how do we make the cross work to get rid of the problem of our self-nature or "flesh?" How can we truly be free?

How do we keep from carrying out the desire of our flesh? We do it by living in the Spirit (Gal. 5:16-18) and crucifying the flesh (Gal. 5:24).

Galatians 5:16-18, 24-25.
16 So I say, live by the Spirit, and you will not gratify the desires of the sinful nature. 17 For the sinful nature desires what is contrary to the Spirit, and the Spirit what is contrary to the sinful nature. They are in conflict with each other, so that you do not do what you want. 18 But if you are led by the Spirit, you are not under law.
24 Those who belong to Christ Jesus have crucified the sinful nature with its passions and desires. 25 Since we live by the Spirit, let us keep in step with the Spirit.

We all want to be dads who exhibit love and joy and peace on a daily basis in every relationship. We want our kids to see us living in peace and harmony with them, with our wives and our co-workers. We want the fruit of the Spirit to flow from us. There is only one way to accomplish that. If we want the Heavenly Vinedresser to enable us to bear more fruit, we will have to let Him get to the root of the problem and cut away with His heavenly pruning shears.

Flesh doesn't need mending. Flesh must die! We don't need to just clean up our flesh; it needs to be crucified.

The principle of the shears: the crucifixion principle

Galatians 2:20

"I have been crucified with Christ; and it is no longer I who live, but Christ lives in me; and the life which I now live in the flesh I live by faith in the Son of God, who loved me, and delivered Himself up for me."

Here it is! Here's the answer to how we can be free! "I am crucified with Christ." Nothing short of death of my fleshy self-nature will set me free. I can't fix it and hope it will get better. I can't use self-help to get stronger. I don't need to learn to cope with it; I need to take it to the cross.

God told the apostle Paul, *"MY strength is made perfect in weakness"* (II Corinthians 12:9). It is not in becoming stronger that I will win the battle over my flesh, it is by coming to the cross and dying that I gain victory.

You don't have to live according to the pull of your flesh. You do not have to be demanding and controlling just because men in your family have "always been that way." You don't have to be weak and passive and let your wife and children run all over you because you've "always been that way." Jesus came to set you free. He died on the cross so that you could live according to His Spirit – His power source – and not your own.

Come to Him today. Come to the cross! Choose this day to "put to death" the deeds of the self-nature. Deal a mortal wound to the flesh. I urge you to get on your knees and lay yourself on His altar.

Lord Jesus Christ, I thank You for Your sacrifice on the cross for me. Now, Lord, I choose to die to my flesh, my self-centered nature.

I don't want my will, Lord, I want Yours and Yours alone. I want to know the truth that will set me free. I pray this in the matchless name of Jesus. Amen.

TIPS FOR DAD

I have a challenge for you, Dad. List your five favorite hobbies...you know, the things you like to do when you are "free." It could be fishing, golfing, watching TV, hunting, basketball, racquetball, etc. Now here is the challenge: Ask yourself, and be very honest: *Would I rather be doing any of these things than being with my wife?* Many times we husbands have a desire to offer sacrificial love, but don't know where to start. This test is a great place to start. The point is that your wife needs to know she is number one in your life. For me, it meant convincing Denise she was more important than all the sports I was playing in as a young husband. But once I convinced her, she ENCOURAGED me to go and play in each of those sports! Do your homework...it's worth it!

DAY 2

WHEN THE CROSS CROSSES YOU

BEGIN WITH PRAYER

Be still and know your Heavenly Father is God. It is He who has made us and not we ourselves. Submit to His authority and humbly bow before Him.

No longer slaves.

Romans 6:4-7.

4 We were therefore buried with him through baptism into death in order that, just as Christ was raised from the dead through the glory of the Father, we too may live a new life.

5 If we have been united with him like this in his death, we will certainly also be united with him in his resurrection. 6 For we know that our old self was crucified with him so that the body of sin might be done away with, that we should no longer be slaves to sin— 7 because anyone who has died has been freed from sin.

There are seven references to death, so we need to pay attention to what has died! The Lord Jesus died, and our old self-nature died. We've been co-crucified with Him. This was so we could be freed from our old self-nature. We're no longer slaves to it.

Romans 6:11-14.

11 In the same way, count yourselves dead to sin but alive to God in Christ Jesus. 12 Therefore do not let sin reign in your mortal body so that you obey its evil desires. 13 Do not offer the parts of your body to sin, as instruments of wickedness, but rather offer yourselves to God, as those who have been brought from death to life; and offer the parts of your body to him as instruments of righteousness. 14 For sin shall not be your master, because you are not under law, but under grace.

I'm dead to sin, alive in Christ. Sin no longer has "lordship" over me. I don't have to obey my fleshy inclination to yell or pout to control others. I can choose to present my mind, body and heart to Jesus so that He can live through me. I'm to "consider myself" dead to sin and *choose* to die to sin. I take myself to the cross.

ACT LIKE WHO YOU ARE. A story is told about Queen Elizabeth. When she was a young teenager, she talked back to her nanny. The nanny grasped her by the shoulders and said, "Do you know who you are? You are the future Queen of England. Now start acting like it!"

It's time we began acting like who we are. We've been freed from the Law of Sin and Death. Jesus paid for our freedom. We're not in bondage to the flesh patterns of our parents or personalities. We're children of the King! We're fathers who have the very life of the Lord Jesus Himself living in us!

ROMANS 8:12-13.

12 Therefore, brothers, we have an obligation—but it is not to the sinful nature, to live according to it. 13 For if you live according to the sinful nature, you will die; but if by the Spirit you put to death the misdeeds of the body, you will live...

The flesh brings death; the Spirit brings life. If I manipulate and control my wife and children to get my needs met, it will create a spiritual deadness in us all. The Spirit is quenched, cutting off the flow of Jesus' life through me. But if I submit myself to the indwelling life of Jesus and let Him guide my wife and children through me, Life will flow from me to my wife and kids. *That's freedom.*

The cross was not just a place in time and history, although it certainly was that. It is also a principle that operates in the life of a believer. This crucifixion principle is "dying to flesh." It's absolutely necessary to obtain the freedom in Christ that we're promised.

When the cross "crosses" you.

If you desire to move forward in knowing Christ Jesus, He will inevitably lead you to the cross. His cross will somehow, someday cross your path. At the place where He crosses you, you'll face a decision. Will I live in the flesh, trying to get what I want, when I want it, the way I want it, or will I choose to go to the cross with what I want and get in on what God wants? May our prayer become like the words of Paul in Philippians 1:21: "*For to me, to live is Christ, and to die is gain.*"

Lord Jesus, keep working. Don't allow me to be satisfied with where I am spiritually. Keep me hungering for more of You. Amen.

TIPS FOR DAD

The first step in setting the boundaries for your child is to carefully explain them. Tell him in a calm but authoritative voice what you expect of him. Get on his level and look him in the eye. Make sure he's focused. Only then will you be able to hold him accountable for first-time obedience. For example, *"John, you must come to me when I call you. When you hear your name, stop what you are doing and come quickly. Don't continue playing or talking. Drop what you are doing and come to me. Don't argue or fuss. Listen to my voice and obey. Do you understand?"* Let John repeat the rule: *"I must come the first time you call me. I must not keep playing."* Then say, *"John, are we really clear about the rule? I don't want you to get in trouble for breaking the rule if you don't understand it."* Let him respond. *"Yes, Dad. I understand the rule."*

DAY 3

THE PLACE OF THE CROSS

BEGIN WITH PRAYER

Ask the Lord to open your understanding of the cross today. Thank Him for all that He did there for you to make you free.

An illustration from Dr. Larry Crabb's book, *The Marriage Builder*[1], may help you better understand the crucifixion principle. Imagine yourself standing at the edge of a cliff.

The cliff of surrender The cliff represents your self-strength and being in control. It feels familiar and safe. You look down into the chasm below and it's frightening. If you were to jump off the cliff, you'd lose control and have to face your fears. You might be rejected or lose the very thing you're holding onto.

Now imagine a rope around your waist – the rope of God's love. It will never fail. Its top is tied securely around Jesus. He's urging you to jump off the cliff of self-strength and hang only by His strength and love. You may look over the edge of the cliff and think, *Wait! What if the rope is too long and I crash at the bottom? Or the rope might break. What if God can't be trusted to really be there?* Most experience the panic of the "hang time" even after we decide to surrender fully to God. It may not seem like He's there. It may not look like He can hold you securely. But if you surrender to Him in total abandon, He'll be there. He Himself has promised, *"I will never desert you, nor will I ever forsake you"* (HEBREWS 13:5).

THE PLACE OF SURRENDER

The cliff represents the "place" of the cross, the place of total surrender. To surrender, you'll have to jump. You'll have to take the leap of faith, letting go of self-reliance and control, and allow Him total control. You will not sense the "power" of the rope... until you jump.

That may mean that you have to let go of fears – fears about finances, a child's safety or future, losing your health, or losing control. Jumping off the cliff of safety may represent letting go of bitterness, anger and unforgiveness. Or it may be letting go of feeding your lustful appetites. God made men with big appetites for power, food, and sex. But are you driven by those desires or by laying your life at the foot of the cross and allowing Christ to satisfy your desires?

When you commit to living the principle of the cross, you'll have to make a decision. It's a crucifixion moment, like jumping off a cliff. You'll have a choice: to jump into God's arms or to stay on the cliff of your own will. Will you let go of all that keeps you from complete dependence on Him?

MATTHEW 10:37-39.

37 "Anyone who loves his father or mother more than me is not worthy of me; anyone who loves his son or daughter more than me is not worthy of me;
38 and anyone who does not take his cross and follow me is not worthy of me.
39 Whoever finds his life will lose it, and whoever loses his life for my sake will find it."

You will never discover life as it was meant to be lived if you don't give in to the cross. You'll never be free to bear the fruit of the Spirit in your children's lives if you resist its call. If you hold on to your self-life, you will lose your whole life. But if you surrender to the cross, you'll find your life. The process begins with the "death" of your will. Then His life will come springing forth.

Lord, I have been crucified with Christ. It is no longer I who live, but You live inside me. Help me to grasp the message of the cross. I am holding tightly to You as I let go of everything else. Amen.

One of the greatest opportunities for family bonding occurs on the family vacation. But this can be a disaster without praying and planning with your wife *and* children. That much "togetherness" can bring out the flesh in us all! So begin early seeking the Lord's direction for the best budget, place and time. Don't miss out on creating lasting memories that will draw your family together...if done His way.

DAY 4

THE PRAYER OF THE CROSS

BEGIN WITH PRAYER

Pray for your wife today. Ask God to anoint her day with blessings, keep her safe, and remove any barriers in her heart to His Word.

God applied the Principle of the Shears, the Crucifixion Principle to the life of His beloved Son for the same reason He applies it to your life. For Jesus to exhibit the full love of the Father's heart for the world, He had to offer His life to the Father. He had to submit to crucifixion so resurrection life could occur for Himself and all who believe in Him. Today, we will look at His trip to the cross, when Jesus was "standing on the cliff" of surrender to the heavenly shears.

Place of decision

Matthew 26:36-39.

36 Then Jesus went with his disciples to a place called Gethsemane, and he said to them, "Sit here while I go over there and pray."

37 He took Peter and the two sons of Zebedee along with him, and he began to be sorrowful and troubled. 38 Then he said to them, "My soul is overwhelmed with sorrow to the point of death. Stay here and keep watch with me."

39 Going a little farther, he fell with his face to the ground and prayed, "My Father, if it is possible, may this cup be taken from me. Yet not as I will, but as you will."

This was Jesus' place of decision. It wasn't easy, but He submitted Himself completely to His Father. If you decide to follow Jesus to the cross, it will not be easy. It will probably be the most challenging thing you've ever done. It will require that you endure pain. It will have a great price tag. It will cost you your life.

LUKE 9:23-25.

23 Then he said to them all: "If anyone would come after me, he must deny himself and take up his cross daily and follow me.

24 For whoever wants to save his life will lose it, but whoever loses his life for me will save it.

25 What good is it for a man to gain the whole world, and yet lose or forfeit his very self?"

Jesus gives three requirements for discipleship: deny yourself; take up your cross daily; and follow Him. If we do so, we'll find life. But if we choose our own way, indulging ourselves however we see fit, we'll lose the very life we're seeking.

Remember MATTHEW 10:37-39?

37 "Anyone who loves his father or mother more than me is not worthy
of me; anyone who loves his son or daughter more than me is not wor-
thy of me; 38 and anyone who does not take his cross and follow me is
not worthy of me. 39 Whoever finds his life will lose it, and whoever
loses his life for my sake will find it."

We must not love anything or anyone more than Christ. What is Jesus is calling you to bring to the cross now? Paul says in GALATIANS 6:14, "*But may it never be that I should boast, except in the cross of our Lord Jesus Christ, through which the world has been crucified to me, and I to the world.*" All in the world was dead to him but Christ.

Journey to the cross. Going to the cross with your fleshy self-nature is not a one-time occurrence. It is the lifestyle of the believer who wants to fully know God.

The first time I was consciously aware of the cross in my life was when I lost my job. When I fell on my face before Christ Jesus, gave up my "right" to financial security, and committed myself to His lordship, it was a crucifixion moment. Another came when it was time to let go of my firstborn, Danielle. I had to give up my "right" to my child and commit her into His hands. There have been many other trips to the cross. Each have been painful. But there's no cure for the flesh except the cross. Nothing but complete surrender to Jesus will bring healing.

It reminds me of going into surgery. You may want to cling to the walls as they roll you down the hall toward the operating room. But once you submit to the process, healing begins. The doctor cuts away the bad and repairs the body, so it can heal.

We can follow Jesus to the cross, or walk in the deadness of the flesh. If we choose to keep company with the flesh for a while, we'll become heart-sick as it begins to rot and stink. Flesh stinks and it's never worth hanging onto.

Has the light begun to dawn on your understanding of the cross? Do you see it as a principle that applies to every facet of your parenting and your life?

Selfer's Prayer

Father, I confess that I've been holding on to my self-strength and trying to live by self-effort, filling my love bucket with relationships, possessions, and prestige. I give up on my self-effort and release my rights and expectations to You. Do with my life what pleases You. I affirm as an act of my will that I've been crucified with Christ, and it is no longer I who live, but Christ who lives in me. Christ is my life. I yield myself to the work of the cross. Bring glory to Yourself through me. In Jesus' name. Amen.

TIPS FOR DAD

List five things about your wife for which you are grateful. Write them down and mail them to her at home. If you're a single dad, list five positive qualities about your ex-wife. Tell your children what you appreciate about their mom.

DAY 5

THE PRACTICE OF THE CROSS

BEGIN WITH PRAYER.

Express to the Lord praise and worship for His holiness. Pray something like, "Lord, You are the holy Lord over all the earth. Glorious is Your matchless name. You are Lord of lords and King of kings, and I worship You."

JOHN 8:28-29.

28 So Jesus said, "When you have lifted up the Son of Man, then you will know that I am the one I claim to be and that I do nothing on my own but speak just what the Father has taught me.

29 The one who sent me is with me; he has not left me alone, for I always do what pleases him."

Jesus lived a life of complete surrender to the Father. He lived the principle of the cross every day of His life on earth before He went to the place of the cross.

The principle of the cross is practical. Understand it, and you will see that it guides every aspect of life. You will begin to recognize the work of the cross in every relationship.

FIRST PRIORITY: RELATIONSHIP WITH GOD. In your relationship with God, there is an overriding principle. It is found in Exodus 20:3, which says, *"You shall have no other gods before Me."*

In this commandment, God establishes His place in our lives. He is priority number one. No other thing in our lives should compete with His place. No relationship, possession, or agenda should become a god to us. He alone is worthy of taking the position of God.

Can you see where the cross crosses you at this point? It is so easy to let the "thorns and thistles" of this world creep into the place of God. We can have a relationship with a spouse or child that turns from pure love to co-dependence. We can get wrapped up in an organization that is "good" but consumes all our energy and time. We can be so in love with a house, car, boat, or vacation place that our lives begin to revolve around keeping it.

And then the cross is presented to us: Will we die to that which we hold so dear, to become alive to where the Spirit is leading? Will we loosen our grip on that which has become "god" to take hold of the true living God of the universe? Is there any relationship or activity or possession God has brought to mind? What is it that has become a god to you?

SECOND PRIORITY: RELATIONSHIP WITH WIFE. The second priority of a father's life is his relationship to his wife. If you're a single dad, please keep reading. These principles are important for dealing with the past as well as leading to the future.

We are commanded numerous times in Scripture to love our wives (EPHESIANS 5:25-28; COLOSSIANS 3:19; I PETER 3:7). It's not vague or ambiguous. It's very clear. The kind of love commanded is sacrificial love; it's the kind of love Christ has for the church in dying for it. Another definition of this kind of love is *giving what is needed without expecting anything in return.* If I believe that definition, then I have to ask myself, what are my wife's needs?

Three Basic Needs of a Wife

The three basic needs of a wife are security, intimate communication, and sincere praise. The *Wisdom for Fathers* Bible study spends a whole week on these important truths in this second most important relationship.

The cross looms before us. Will I go to the cross with my self-centered attitudes and critical tongue? Will I choose to put off pride and stubbornness, and to put on humility and meekness? Do you see the cross before you as it crosses the path of your marriage?

Take a few moments to pray right now. Ask God to speak to you about your marriage in a way you can hear and understand Him. Listen to His voice and obey.

Third Priority: Relationship with Children.

The third priority of a father's life is his relationship to his children. There are three gifts that I believe every father should give his children (for a more complete study see *Wisdom for Fathers*). These gifts are to be given in order. The first gift a father needs to give his children is the gift of unconditional love.

Gift One: Unconditional Love

Read I Corinthians 13:1-8. Where you see the word *love,* insert the words "unconditional love for *(child's name)*." Did the cross cross your path? Did you see where God's unconditional love for your child and your love for your child are out of alignment?

Gift Two: Firm and Fair Discipline

Proverbs 19:18 says, "*Discipline your son while there is hope, and do not desire his death.*" If we don't discipline our kids, we may be a willing party to their death! That's strong language!

Gift Three: The Bread of Life

The third gift a father should give his child is the *Bread of Life,* the Word of God.

To share Christ with our kids, we must first live our own life transparently and honestly, seeking God with total abandon. Have you ever been around someone who lives like that? The power of the life of Jesus operates through them in such fullness that it is contagious. You just want what they have. Our children are looking into our faces to see if they can find the face of the Heavenly Father. What will they see in your face?

We should expose our children to the Word of God. While it is important to take them to Bible classes at church on a regular basis, remember that nothing replaces what they learn at home. The home is their laboratory for the Bible. When your child is afraid in the middle of the night, he can most readily learn, *"When I am afraid, I will put my trust in You"* (Psalm 56:3).

When your teenager is overwhelmed with research paper deadlines, play-off games, "love" interests, and college applications, *"Cast your burden upon the Lord and He will sustain you"* (Psalm 55:22) will mean more to him.

Finally, pray with and pray for your children. From the time they are toddlers in high chairs, begin teaching your child to pray. Say a simple prayer and let him pray it phrase by phrase after you. Pray over him at bedtime. Let your words in prayer be the last thing he hears before he goes to sleep.

When your children are older, you will be blessed at the joy of having a family prayer time. Set aside a time each week to pray with your children over the issues they're facing. Children need to see your spiritual leadership in the home, Dad. You need to set the example of total dependence on the Lord.

Deuteronomy 6:1-8.

1 These are the commands, decrees and laws the LORD your God directed me to teach you to observe in the land that you are crossing the Jordan to possess, 2 so that you, your children and their children after them may fear the LORD your God as long as you live by keeping all his decrees and commands that I give you, and so that you may enjoy long life. 3 Hear, O Israel, and be careful to obey so that it may go well with you and that you may increase greatly in a land flowing with milk and honey, just as the LORD, the God of your fathers, promised you.

4 Hear, O Israel: The LORD our God, the LORD is one. 5 Love the LORD your God with all your heart and with all your soul and with all your strength. 6 These commandments that I give you today are to be upon your hearts. 7 Impress them on your children. Talk about them when you sit at home and when you walk along the road, when you lie down and when you get up. 8 Tie them as symbols on your hands and bind them on your foreheads.

Pay special attention to the generational blessing of verses 1-3, as well as the "transfer of the baton faith" in verses 7-8. Did the cross come into view when you thought of how your children are being trained in matters of faith? Is Jesus speaking to your heart concerning your diligence in this vital responsibility?

Fourth priority: your work

The fourth priority of a father's life is his work. This may surprise you. Work is my fourth priority? Yeah, guys. Tune in now. What's coming up next is important.

God created man to be the protector and provider for the home. So it's unfortunate that many men, after "conquering" their mate in marriage, ignore their wives to go on to their next conquest: their work. As a result, work becomes more and more important, to the detriment of their family.

God gave work to man in the very beginning, when Adam was assigned to take care of the Garden of Eden (GENESIS 2:15). So work is a good thing, given by God for man. Even after the Fall, when pain and frustration came with labor, work itself remained good. We get in trouble when we work for the wrong reasons. Our society has devised a mindset which holds out the promise that work will give us wealth, prestige, esteem, purpose, values, standards, and success. But God never intended for us to work for these reasons.[2] Our work is to express the giftedness God gave us, not to get our personal needs met. Our work is to glorify God and be another place where we can express His life. No matter what work you are involved in, this is your reason for working.

Reflect on the cross. Does anything about your work or play habits need to go to the cross? How did you do on your tests?

FIFTH PRIORITY: YOUR MINISTRY. The fifth priority of a father's life is his relationship with the world through his ministry.

JEREMIAH 18:1-6.

1 This is the word that came to Jeremiah from the LORD: 2 "Go down
to the potter's house, and there I will give you my message." 3 So I went
down to the potter's house, and I saw him working at the wheel. 4 But
the pot he was shaping from the clay was marred in his hands; so the
potter formed it into another pot, shaping it as seemed best to him.
5 Then the word of the LORD came to me: 6 "O house of Israel, can I
not do with you as this potter does?" declares the LORD. "Like clay in
the hand of the potter, so are you in my hand, O house of Israel.

The key word to the fifth priority is to *yield*. The clay must yield to the potter's hand as he shapes and molds the clay to be used as a vessel. The beginning of ministry is yieldedness to God. It is answering *yes* to Him before you know the question.

Putting off the old, putting on the new

Colossians 3:5-10.

5 Put to death, therefore, whatever belongs to your earthly nature: sexual immorality, impurity, lust, evil desires and greed, which is idolatry. 6 Because of these, the wrath of God is coming. 7 You used to walk in these ways, in the life you once lived. 8 But now you must rid yourselves of all such things as these: anger, rage, malice, slander, and filthy language from your lips. 9 Do not lie to each other, since you have taken off your old self with its practices 10 and have put on the new self, which is being renewed in knowledge in the image of its Creator.

Compare these verses with the act of putting on and taking off clothing.

Why don't you spend a few moments in prayer now? As if you are taking off layers of clothing, consciously take off and "lay aside" the five filthy, fleshy garments listed in Colossians 3:8 that do not belong on a child of God. Specifically pray this prayer in regard to your relationship with your children. Your prayer may go something like this:

Lord, I am taking off the garment of anger right now. As an act of my will, I die to any anger that is in my heart toward my child or anyone else. I choose to forgive them of wrongdoing. I choose today to "put on" Your unconditional love, whether or not I feel like being loving.

Go through each fleshy attitude listed in VERSE 8 and pray a similar prayer, making it personal to your situation.

I JOHN 3:14-16.

14 We know that we have passed from death to life, because we love our brothers. Anyone who does not love remains in death. 15 Anyone who hates his brother is a murderer, and you know that no murderer has eternal life in him.

16 This is how we know what love is: Jesus Christ laid down his life for us. And we ought to lay down our lives for our brothers.

Where does the cross fit in this picture? Do you see it? Where are you being asked to lay down your "life" in ministry?

Only when the cross becomes the power base of your relationship with your children will you experience fathering as it is intended in the heart of God. A father who willingly goes to the cross with his flesh is one whose children can experience the life of Jesus in tangible form. They see His eyes looking out through your eyes. They hear His voice in the firm but gentle tones of your voice. They feel the touch of His hands and the caress of His arms through your touch. It is all accomplished when a father goes to the cross.

Lord, I see the cross more clearly now. It has crossed my life many times. Make me aware when your cross crosses my will. I surrender my will to Your will, to be Yours alone. In Jesus' name. Amen.

TIPS FOR DAD

Finish these statements: "My dreams for our future are..."

"The most wonderful thing my wife ever did for me was..."

"What I've learned from my wife over the years is..."

Share these over a romantic dinner with your wife. Buy her flowers, take her to a romantic restaurant, or create your own romantic environment at home. They never get enough of that!

WEEKEND STUDY

FLESH PATTERNS

If you had trouble recognizing flesh in yourself, you might just read through the list below. If any of these things sound like you, then take time today to take it to the cross as you kneel in prayer.

Flesh Patterns

Anger	Impulsiveness	Anxiety
Inadequacy	Argumentativeness	Bigotry
Indifference	Insecurity	Boasting
Laziness	Being a Loner	Bossiness
Materialism	Negativism	Causing Dissension
Controlling	Opinionated	Conceited
Overly sensitive	Hatred	Critical tongue
Overly submissive	Depression	Passivity
Envy	Pride	Undue sadness
Fear	Profane	Resentment
Feelings of Rejection	Gluttony	Rebellion at authority
Gluttony	Feeling worthless	Self-centeredness
Idolatry	Self-confidence	Impure thoughts
Self-depreciation	Impatience	Self-hatred
Self-indulgence	Slow to forgive	Self-justification
Stubbornness	Self-pity	Self-reliance
Too quick to speak	Quick-temper	Self-righteousness
Vanity	Workaholic	Self-sufficiency
Withdrawal	Sensuality	Selfish-ambition
Sexual lust	Worry[5]	

I am learning to submit to the way of the cross more readily. Day by day, I am learning that when something crosses me, and I begin to fret that I am not getting my way, that something is the cross. And I have a decision to make. I can take the leap off the cliff into the arms of God, or I can hold onto my feeble, self-produced security.

Do you have a child who is giving you trouble and embarrassing you? What flesh patterns is Jesus exposing in you? Prideful flesh? Controlling flesh? Fearful flesh?

Do you have a child who refuses to obey when you call? What flesh patterns is Jesus revealing in you? Passive, fearful flesh? People-pleasing flesh? Lazy flesh?

Do you have a child who is begging for attention by being sick, whining or irritating others, or failing in school? What flesh patterns is Jesus revealing in you? Self-centered, self-absorbed flesh? Or the opposite, over-protective flesh?

Your child's sinful, fleshy behavior is not your fault. He has his own will, but you are responsible before God for your response to your child's behavior. When your child embarrasses you by acting out in front of your friends, do you act out of your pride and try to cover it up with an excuse? *"He's just tired,"* or *"She's been sick."* Do you yell or use guilt or fear to try to control him, just to make yourself look better? Do you collapse in fear at what he might do if you really discipline him?

Or are you ready to take those issues to the cross for crucifixion, so that Jesus' life can be borne out through you to deal with your child in the Spirit? Remember, you can discipline a child with a rod "in the flesh" or discipline him with a rod "in the Spirit." You can set boundaries for a teenager "in the flesh" or set boundaries for him "in the Spirit." Do you see the difference?

I am praying for you. I know by experience how challenging being the spiritual leader of your home can be. You and I are on a very important lesson plan written just for us by our Heavenly Father. He knew exactly which father to place with which child to expose and reveal flesh, and once clean, to pour out His life. Come to Jesus. Jump off the cliff and jump into His arms, where true freedom and real life begins.

For those who are seeking a first time relationship with Christ:

John 15:1-6.

1 "I am the true vine, and my Father is the gardener. 2 He cuts off every branch in me that bears no fruit, while every branch that does bear fruit he prunes so that it will be even more fruitful. 3 You are already clean because of the word I have spoken to you. 4 Remain in me, and I will remain in you. No branch can bear fruit by itself; it must remain in the vine. Neither can you bear fruit unless you remain in me.

5 "I am the vine; you are the branches. If a man remains in me and I in him, he will bear much fruit; apart from me you can do nothing. 6 If anyone does not remain in me, he is like a branch that is thrown away and withers; such branches are picked up, thrown into the fire and burned.

Jesus' words to those who do not bear fruit at all are very strong. He says that those who are not receiving their life from the Vine and bearing fruit will be taken away, cast into the fire and burned. What is Jesus saying? Those who do not know Him as Savior of their lives, who have not asked forgiveness for their sins and have not asked Him into their hearts, will die and go to hell. Hell is a very real place. God did not create it for human beings, He created it for Satan and his demonic angels. But Jesus' words are chillingly clear. If a man or woman refuses His way of salvation, they will die in their sins. And the penalty for dying a sinner is eternal hell.

"He made Him who knew no sin to be sin on our behalf, that we might become the righteousness of God in Him" (II CORINTHIANS 5:21). Jesus exchanged His sinless life for your sinful life. He took your sin, so you could take His righteousness. But you must receive it as a conscious choice. It does not happen to you because you were raised in a Christian home. You do not escape hell because you go to church. You must recognize that you are a sinner and ask forgiveness for your sins. You need to pray a prayer something like:

Lord, I am a sinner. I need a Savior. Please forgive my sins and enter my heart as Master, Lord and Savior. I want to become Your child. Thank You for dying on the cross for me. Please count Your death as the payment for my sins. In the name of Jesus. Amen.

If you prayed that prayer, call your pastor or Christian friend. You need to share this good news with someone today! You are now God's child! You are in the family! You are born again—you are saved! Write out today's date so you will always remember this historic day in your life!

Notes

[1] *The Marriage Builder,* Dr. Larry Crabb, Zondervan Publishers, 1992. Illustration used by permission.

[2] *Why Go to Work?,* Ministry in the Marketplace Series, Vision Foundation, Inc., Knoxville, Tennessee, 1987, p 9.

WEEK 5

THE PRINCIPLE OF THE SHEARS: CUTTING AWAY

Letting go and letting God control our circumstances is often hard for dads. I'll begin this unit with a personal story that may help...

FatherWise Group Prayer Requests

The first person in the group will share a one sentence prayer request about his wife or his children. Each person in the group will pray a one sentence prayer over that request before moving on to the next person's request. The group will continue in this way until everyone has prayed over each request.

DAY 1

THE PICTURE OF THE CROSS

BEGIN WITH PRAYER

Pray today for your children. Ask God to give each one a hunger for His Word and to fill them with His presence.

On January 1, 1993, I went into our study for my "special quïet time." On New Year's Day I dedicate more time and attention to seeking the Lord. I write in my prayer journal on these occasions so I can look back and see God's work.

At that time, my career as a geophysicist for an oil company was uncertain. I sensed God speaking about this. I wrote: "Lord, You have brought to my attention EPHESIANS 5:15, *'Be very careful, then, how you live—not as unwise but as wise, making the most of every opportunity because the days are evil'* (NIV)." I was sure God was going to give us some kind of opportunity in 1993. I wrote three prayers of "resolution" to be delivered from: the stronghold of fear; a critical attitude; and the "the love of money."

God wasted no time challenging me. Within six weeks I was laid off from my job. For a man with a stronghold of fear, it was devastating. The next weekend, Denise and I borrowed a friend's lake house. For 24 hours, we did nothing but read Scripture, pray and share. It was intense. We read the story in 2 KINGS 4:1-7 about the widow and the jars of oil. God showed us that we must be empty vessels for Him to fill us with His oil, the Holy Spirit.

Later, a pastor friend suggested a seminar based on the book *Handbook to Happiness.*[1] As I attended and read, the reality of my need to "go to the cross" sank in. God was saying something powerful. I grew uncomfortable as I realized going to the cross "means surrender with no reservations—not friends, family, profession, future, possessions. Anything that we are or have or might be is included in such a complete surrender. If we are dead serious, we are going to be seriously dead! Our surrender is basically our permission for our Father to take us to the cross."[2]

Losing a job, profession and possessions didn't seem as hard as surrendering my family. I was emotional considering the cost of releasing them, giving God the right to use their lives any way He chose. I knew Christ had died on the cross for me 2000 years ago, but the principle of my co-crucifixion with Him now became very clear.

GALATIANS 2:20.
I have been crucified with Christ and I no longer live, but Christ lives in me. The life I live in the body, I live by faith in the Son of God, who loved me and gave himself for me.

I had to die to my self-nature. On the cliff of safety, I heard God say "Jump!" A major flesh war was raging: If you jump, you'll be completely out of control. This is ME being crucified! But with the job loss, the intense prayer, and the principle stated so clearly in GALATIANS 2:20, God had prepared me. So on March 11, 1993, I got on my knees and prayed the Selfer's Prayer. I was saved from sin when I was 11 years old. Now, I was being saved from my self-nature.

After this trip to the cross, the fear and insecurity of the job loss disappeared. Why? Because I was no longer depending on "self" to provide, and I now understood I had no "rights" to an easy, comfortable life. I realized if I needed to be jobless for God to teach me, then that's what I wanted. When you're dead to your own agenda, you can pray in the midst of suffering, "Lord don't stop until I've learned all You want me to learn."

Paul says it best in PHILIPPIANS 3:7-8: "*But whatever things were gain to me, those things I have counted as loss for the sake of Christ. More than that, I count all things to be loss in view of the surpassing value of knowing Christ Jesus my Lord, for whom I have suffered the loss of all things, and count them but rubbish so that I may gain Christ...*"

Pray those words to God now; releasing "whatever things" He brings to mind.

TIPS FOR DAD

Are you and your wife a "united front" to your children concerning discipline and setting boundaries? Spend some time together discussing rules and consequences you want to establish in your home. Discuss how you can optimize each of your parenting strengths and overcome your parenting weaknesses.

DAY 2

THE PERSONAL CALL OF THE CROSS

BEGIN WITH PRAYER

Offer a personal time of praise and adoration to the Heavenly Father. Thank Him for the events and circumstances of your life that draw you near to Him and His life in you.

Once a little peach seed lived in a drawer in the master gardener's shed.[3] He waited and waited to be chosen by the master. Finally one day, the master opened the drawer and chose him. Placing the little seed on his hand, the gardener started walking out into the sunshine.

The little seed was so proud. He's chosen me! He looked smugly about the garden to make sure all the other plants saw him. The gardener knelt down on one knee and began to dig a small hole. The hole got deeper and deeper as the gardener continued to dig. When he was finished digging the gardener took the little seed and placed it in the bottom of the hole.

The seed looked up and thought, It's dark in here, and it's a little damp. But if this is where the gardener wants to put me, I trust him. He knows what he's doing. Then the gardener took a hand full of dirt and threw it in on top of the seed. The seed wiped his eyes and said, "You just threw dirt in my face!" About that time the gardener threw a little more dirt in. The seed called out, "Hey, this is me, the one you chose. Stop throwing that dirt down here!" But the gardener continued to pile more and more dirt into the hole. As the hole completely filled up, the gardener took his boot and tamped down the dirt to compress it into the little seed.

Have you ever felt like that little seed in the Heavenly Gardener's hand?

John 12:24-26

I tell you the truth, unless a kernel of wheat falls to the ground and dies, it remains only a single seed. But if it dies, it produces many seeds. The man who loves his life will lose it, while the man who hates his life in this world will keep it for eternal life. Whoever serves me must follow me; and where I am, my servant also will be. My Father will honor the one who serves me."

John 12:27 through John 13:3.

27 "Now my heart is troubled, and what shall I say? 'Father, save me
from this hour'? No, it was for this very reason I came to this hour. 28
Father, glorify your name!" Then a voice came from heaven, "I have
glorified it, and will glorify it again." 29 The crowd that was there
and heard it said it had thundered; others said an angel had spoken
to him.

30 Jesus said, "This voice was for your benefit, not mine. 31 Now is the
time for judgment on this world; now the prince of this world will be
driven out. 32 But I, when I am lifted up from the earth, will draw all
men to myself." 33 He said this to show the kind of death he was going
to die.

34 The crowd spoke up, "We have heard from the Law that the Christ
will remain forever, so how can you say, 'The Son of Man must be
lifted up'? Who is this 'Son of Man'?"

35 Then Jesus told them, "You are going to have the light just a little
while longer. Walk while you have the light, before darkness overtakes
you. The man who walks in the dark does not know where he is going.
36 Put your trust in the light while you have it, so that you may be-

come sons of light." When he had finished speaking, Jesus left and hid himself from them.

37 Even after Jesus had done all these miraculous signs in their presence, they still would not believe in him. 38 This was to fulfill the word of Isaiah the prophet:

"Lord, who has believed our message and to whom has the arm of the Lord been revealed?"

39 For this reason they could not believe, because, as Isaiah says elsewhere:

40 "He has blinded their eyes and deadened their hearts, so they can neither see with their eyes, nor understand with their hearts, nor turn—and I would heal them."

41 Isaiah said this because he saw Jesus' glory and spoke about him.

42 Yet at the same time many even among the leaders believed in him. But because of the Pharisees they would not confess their faith for fear they would be put out of the synagogue; 43 for they loved praise from men more than praise from God.

44 Then Jesus cried out, "When a man believes in me, he does not believe in me only, but in the one who sent me. 45 When he looks at me, he sees the one who sent me. 46 I have come into the world as a light, so that no one who believes in me should stay in darkness.

47 "As for the person who hears my words but does not keep them, I do not judge him. For I did not come to judge the world, but to save it. 48 There is a judge for the one who rejects me and does not accept my words; that very word which I spoke will condemn him at the last day. 49 For I did not speak of my own accord, but the Father who sent me commanded me what to say and how to say it. 50 I know that his command leads to eternal life. So whatever I say is just what the Father has told me to say."

John 13: 1-3

1 It was just before the Passover Feast. Jesus knew that the time had come for him to leave this world and go to the Father. Having loved his own who were in the world, he now showed them the full extent of his love.

2 The evening meal was being served, and the devil had already prompted Judas Iscariot, son of Simon, to betray Jesus.

3 Jesus knew that the Father had put all things under his power, and that he had come from God and was returning to God;

When Jesus spoke these words, He was on His way to the cross. He called to His disciples to follow Him there. Now He is calling your name, asking you to follow Him to the cross. It is there that flesh and sin must die. *"If anyone would come after me, he must deny himself and take up his cross and follow me"* (Matthew 16:24).

We must take a hard look at the cross of Jesus. What is Jesus asking of us? Where will this cross experience take us? The cross is not an event that only existed in time and space; it is an eternal principle. The indwelling cross in me is an internal altar where I sacrifice my will to His will, my wants for His wants.

Jesus, I want to follow You. I give up all that has kept me from total surrender to Your will. Hear my heart's cry, Lord. Amen.

TIPS FOR DAD

Have a heart-to-heart talk with your wife. Listen to her; don't talk until she is through talking. Ask questions and listen as if you were going to be tested on every detail. This is probably the greatest gift you could ever give her.

DAY 3

THE PROOF OF THE CROSS

BEGIN WITH PRAYER

Pray for your church, pastor and staff. Ask the Lord to shield and protect your church from attacks from Satan. Ask Him to empty your pastor of his flesh and fill him with the life of Jesus. Ask God to bring about revival and repentance.

THE FIRST MARTYR. When the cross is present in the life of a believer, his life takes on a decided difference. No one is able to be in his company without being affected by it. The life of one of the disciples of Jesus was such a life. He stands tall above the rest.

ACTS 6:8-15.

"Now Stephen, a man full of God's grace and power, did great wonders and miraculous signs among the people. But some men from what was called the Synagogue of the Freedmen, including both Cyrenians and Alexandrians, and some from Cilicia and Asia, rose up and argued with Stephen. And yet they were unable to cope with the wisdom and the Spirit with which he was speaking. Then they secretly induced men to say, 'We have heard him speak blasphemous words against Moses and against God.' And they stirred up the people, the elders and the scribes, and they came upon him and dragged him away, and brought him before the Council. And they put forward false witnesses who said, 'This man incessantly speaks against this holy place, and the Law; for we have heard him say that this Nazarene, Jesus, will destroy this place and alter the customs which Moses handed down to us.' And fixing

their gaze on him, all who were sitting in the Council saw his face like the face of an angel."

The principle of the cross led Stephen to witness to the Jews, knowing what he would endure because of his preaching. The place of the cross came for Stephen in a showdown with the Jewish council. The presence of the cross made Stephen's face shine on the outside because of the glory within. But did the cross keep Stephen from experiencing difficulties? Hardly!

Acts 7:54-60.

54 When they heard this, they were furious and gnashed their teeth at
him. 55 But Stephen, full of the Holy Spirit, looked up to heaven and
saw the glory of God, and Jesus standing at the right hand of God. 56
"Look," he said, "I see heaven open and the Son of Man standing at the
right hand of God."

57 At this they covered their ears and, yelling at the top of their voices,
they all rushed at him, 58 dragged him out of the city and began to
stone him. Meanwhile, the witnesses laid their clothes at the feet of a
young man named Saul.

59 While they were stoning him, Stephen prayed, "Lord Jesus, receive
my spirit." 60 Then he fell on his knees and cried out, "Lord, do not
hold this sin against them." When he had said this, he fell asleep.

Stephen entered into the fellowship of Jesus' suffering by giving up his life. The cross cost him dearly. But do you know what happened as a result of Stephen's martyrdom? Christianity spread from Jerusalem into the entire world. The disciples of Jesus, running for their lives took the gospel message into every part of the earth. Kingdom fruit was born out of Stephen's ultimate sacrifice.

The fact that you are reading this Christian book written by a Gentile author 2000 years after the event is a result of the indwelling cross of Christ in the life of Stephen. One disciple took seriously the message of the cross, and the world will never be the same. That is the power of the cross.

Will you allow the presence of the cross into your life? Will you commit to laying down your life "for your friends?" Will you follow the cross at any cost to yourself? Will you be the kernel of wheat that falls to the ground and dies, that it may bear much fruit?

Lord, give me the grace to follow the cross. I open my heart and ask you now to plant the cross there. Have mercy on me and give me the courage to follow You at any cost. I ask all of this in the name that is above every name. And that name is Jesus. Amen.

TIPS FOR DAD

Because dads are called upon to be the providers and protectors of our families, you might have a tendency to be very "performance oriented." Christ accepts you not for how you perform, but for who you are. As a father, it's critical to accept our children for who they are, not for how they perform. Measuring performance is a necessity in our schools and work, but we must accept our children just like the Heavenly Father accepts us, regardless of performance. Ask God to show you how to be more loving and accepting of your children.

DAY 4

THE POWER OF THE CROSS

BEGIN WITH PRAYER

Come before the Lord on behalf of your children today. Pray that they will know the power of the cross.

Fruit trees produce fruit after their kind: apple trees produce apples, and orange trees produce oranges. Fruit is an outward sign of the life within the tree. Believers also produce fruit in keeping with the life within.

We've studied the principle of the cross, the place of the cross, the practice of the cross, and the presence of the cross. Today, we will see that the power of the cross is the evidence that the work of the cross is complete.

The power of the cross is the way God works through believers. When we take the cross to heart, God can work through us to reach another heart that's ready for the cross.

II Corinthians 4:7-18.

7 But we have this treasure in jars of clay to show that this all-sur-
passing power is from God and not from us. 8 We are hard pressed
on every side, but not crushed; perplexed, but not in despair; 9 per-
secuted, but not abandoned; struck down, but not destroyed. 10 We
always carry around in our body the death of Jesus, so that the life of
Jesus may also be revealed in our body. 11 For we who are alive are
always being given over to death for Jesus' sake, so that his life may

be revealed in our mortal body. 12 So then, death is at work in us, but life is at work in you.

13 It is written: "I believed; therefore I have spoken." With that same spirit of faith we also believe and therefore speak, 14 because we know that the one who raised the Lord Jesus from the dead will also raise us with Jesus and present us with you in his presence. 15 All this is for your benefit, so that the grace that is reaching more and more people may cause thanksgiving to overflow to the glory of God.

16 Therefore we do not lose heart. Though outwardly we are wasting away, yet inwardly we are being renewed day by day. 17 For our light and momentary troubles are achieving for us an eternal glory that far outweighs them all. 18 So we fix our eyes not on what is seen, but on what is unseen. For what is seen is temporary, but what is unseen is eternal.

In these verses, we see that our power source is in Christ; it is not in ourselves. It enables someone like Stephen to *"carry about in his body the dying of Jesus so that the life of Jesus might be manifested in his body."*

The definition of the exchanged life is that I die to my self-life so that Christ's life can be lived out in me. I exchange the old nature for the new one.

One of the benefits of paying the cost of the cross is that through our dying to our self-life, others can share in the grace of Jesus Christ. The ultimate reward for exchanging my life for His life is that I can know Christ and the power of His resurrection. I can see Him in a way I could not if I held onto my self-strength and self-sufficiency.

Imagine that you and your children are the only people in the world. Now re-read II Corinthians 4:7-18 and insert your name every time Paul uses the words "we" or "our" or "us." Insert your children's names when he is speaking to the Corinthians using the words you or yours. I've written the first few verses with our names as an example for you:

"But I, David have this treasure in my earthen vessel, that the surpassing greatness of the power may be of God and not from myself; I, David am afflicted in every way, but not crushed; perplexed, but not despairing; persecuted, but not forsaken; struck down, but not destroyed; always carrying about in the body the dying of Jesus, that the life of Jesus also may be manifested in my body. For I, David, who lives is constantly being delivered over to death for Jesus' sake, that the life of Jesus also may be manifested in my mortal flesh. So death works in me, David, but life in Danielle, Cliff, Stephanie, Micah, Brittany and Aaron."

Do you and I really want to produce godly offspring? Do we want to see our children producing fruit in the kingdom? Then it'll cost something. It will require a trip to the cross.

Lord, I'm willing to carry about in my body the dying of Jesus so that the life of Jesus may be manifested in me. Lord, use me as Your instrument in my children's lives to accomplish Your purpose. Enable me to love, discipline and lead them to You according to Your plan for each one. Let me see them through Your eyes. Amen.

TIPS FOR DAD

Gather the family at the table and get a pack of Post-It Notes. Let family members suggest alternatives to watching TV. Stick the notes on the television. When someone in the family is tempted to "veg" in front of the TV, have them close their eyes and pick a note. Some suggestions are: Read; Draw/color; Phone grandparents or other family members; Put on a puppet show; Make cookies; Take a walk or bike ride; Play a game; Draw on the sidewalk with sidewalk chalk; Listen to music; Take a nap.

DAY 5

THE PRODUCE OF THE CROSS

BEGIN WITH PRAYER

Ask the Father to carry out the work of the cross in your life. Ask Him to cross your life with the cross.

Let's pick up Stephen's story from Day 3 to see the power of the cross in his life, as it intersects another young man's life.

READ ACTS 7:58-60.

58 [they] dragged him [Steven] out of the city and began to stone him.
Meanwhile, the witnesses laid their clothes at the feet of a young man
named Saul. 59 While they were stoning him, Stephen prayed, "Lord
Jesus, receive my spirit." 60 Then he fell on his knees and cried out,
"Lord, do not hold this sin against them." When he had said this, he
fell asleep.

Stephen had been at the height of his ministry, performing great wonders and signs among the people. Before his death, he argued with men from Asia and Cilicia. Tarsus, Saul's town, was the key city in Cilicia. Perhaps Saul had argued with Stephen and lost because he was unable to cope with the wisdom and Spirit with which Stephen spoke. It's no wonder he stood by triumphantly as Stephen's murderers laid their garments at his feet.

But don't you imagine that the lovely face of Stephen would not leave Saul's mind? The pure sacrifice of that life must have haunted his dreams and driven him to wipe it out of his mind.

Acts 8:1-3.

1 On that day a great persecution broke out against the church at Jerusalem, and all except the apostles were scattered throughout Judea and Samaria. 2 Godly men buried Stephen and mourned deeply for him. 3 But Saul began to destroy the church. Going from house to house, he dragged off men and women and put them in prison.

Acts 9:1-18.

1 Meanwhile, Saul was still breathing out murderous threats against the Lord's disciples. He went to the high priest 2 and asked him for letters to the synagogues in Damascus, so that if he found any there who belonged to the Way, whether men or women, he might take them as prisoners to Jerusalem.

3 As he neared Damascus on his journey, suddenly a light from heaven flashed around him.

4 He fell to the ground and heard a voice say to him, "Saul, Saul, why do you persecute me?"

5 "Who are you, Lord?" Saul asked.

"I am Jesus, whom you are persecuting," he replied. 6 "Now get up and go into the city, and you will be told what you must do."

7 The men traveling with Saul stood there speechless; they heard the sound but did not see anyone. 8 Saul got up from the ground, but when he opened his eyes he could see nothing. So they led him by the hand into Damascus. 9 For three days he was blind, and did not eat or drink anything.

10 In Damascus there was a disciple named Ananias. The Lord called to him in a vision, "Ananias!"

"Yes, Lord," he answered.

11 The Lord told him, "Go to the house of Judas on Straight Street and ask for a man from Tarsus named Saul, for he is praying. 12 In a vision he has seen a man named Ananias come and place his hands on him to restore his sight."

13 "Lord," Ananias answered, "I have heard many reports about this *man and all the harm he has done to your saints in Jerusalem. 14 And he has come here with authority from the chief priests to arrest all who call on your name."*

15 But the Lord said to Ananias, "Go! This man is my chosen instrument to carry my name before the Gentiles and their kings and before the people of Israel. 16 I will show him how much he must suffer for my name."

17 Then Ananias went to the house and entered it. Placing his hands on Saul, he said, "Brother Saul, the Lord—Jesus, who appeared to you on the road as you were coming here—has sent me so that you may see again and be filled with the Holy Spirit."18 Immediately, something like scales fell from Saul's eyes, and he could see again. He got up and was baptized,

When Jesus addressed Saul, He said, "Why are you persecuting Me?" Jesus was already ascended to the Father, so Jesus was referring to His life being lived out in the life of Stephen and the other disciples. When Stephen laid down his life, it allowed the power of the cross to reach Saul. Then Saul took the gospel outside the walls of Judaism to the Gentiles.

Now read what Saul (whose name was changed to Paul) wrote in COLOSSIANS 1:24-29.

24 Now I rejoice in what was suffered for you, and I fill up in my flesh what is still lacking in regard to Christ's afflictions, for the sake of his body, which is the church. 25 I have become its servant by the commission God gave me to present to you the word of God in its fullness— 26 the mystery that has been kept hidden for ages and generations, but is now disclosed to the saints. 27 To them God has chosen to make known among the Gentiles the glorious riches of this mystery, which is Christ in you, the hope of glory. 28 We proclaim him, admonishing and teaching everyone with all wisdom, so that we may present everyone perfect in Christ. 29 To this end I labor, struggling with all his energy, which so powerfully works in me.

Can you believe this is the same man who watched Stephen's stoning? His words sound like they could have been Stephen's. Do you see that Stephen's sacrifice was one of the things that resulted in the power of the cross moving in Paul's life?

To fully realize the power of the cross, you must adopt the Principle of the Cross as a way of life. Dying to self and living to Jesus must be as constant as breathing out and breathing in. The place of the cross will one day cross your path. To fully realize the power of the cross, you must align your will with the Father's in that critical time and place where there will be a crucifixion moment of decision.

You have an opportunity to practice the full power of the cross each day as you walk in brokenness with God, your family, and the world. The presence of the cross's power in your life will be revealed in the window of your eyes and the glow on your face. The awesome, dynamic power of the cross will reach beyond you into the hearts and lives of those who will see it in your life and be forever changed.

In this week's Weekend Study lesson you will see the "Signs of Brokenness" list. It will show you if you've made your trip to the cross.

Lord, I offer my heart as a living sacrifice. Place the cross upon my heart. I die to self and flesh and sin and I live to You alone. Pour out Your life into mine. In the holy name of Jesus I pray. Amen.

TIPS FOR DAD

Denise and I did not allow our girls to call boys. This temptation can start in elementary school, but it's an epidemic by junior high. In an effort to be popular, many parents even encourage this practice. We believe allowing this can start the male-female relationship too early and on the wrong foot, undermining the biblical example of the male being the head of the home (Col. 11:3). Dad, don't allow your boys to receive calls from girls. Teach them to explain the rules of your house to any girl who calls on them. The best way to teach your "maturing children" how to treat the opposite sex is by your personal example. The way you treat your wife speaks louder than any words you could say. Your girls and boys need to see the gentlemanly way you treat your wife: opening her car door; being polite, protective, and caring; treating her like a queen. That's the way we want the guys to treat the girls, and we want the girls to expect that from the guys. It's an awesome responsibility Dads...only Christ can do it through you!

WEEKEND STUDY

THE PRODUCE OF THE CROSS

The great truths God taught me through the job loss I described in Day 1 eluded me for 32 years. They had been there in Scripture all along, but perhaps my flesh didn't want to hear it. My heart's cry to you, Dad, is to not miss this. The empowerment you need to be a godly father can only be accomplished in the resurrection power of the cross...and that's the catch. You must go to the cross before there can be resurrection power.

PHILIPPIANS 3:8-10.

8 What is more, I consider everything a loss compared to the surpassing greatness of knowing Christ Jesus my Lord, for whose sake I have lost all things. I consider them rubbish, that I may gain Christ 9 and be found in him, not having a righteousness of my own that comes from the law, but that which is through faith in Christ—the righteousness that comes from God and is by faith. 10 I want to know Christ and the power of his resurrection and the fellowship of sharing in his sufferings, becoming like him in his death...

In VERSE 10, he gives the reason that he can joyfully give everything up to Christ: "*...that I may know Him and the power of His resurrection and the fellowship of His suffering, being conformed to His death...*"

Once I began to allow Christ to live in me instead of relying on my own strength, I suddenly sensed a new freedom in living I had never understood before. My hang-ups about being in control, always being right, being super-critical, and having the love of money for my personal security slowly began to change. I began to see money more as God's instrument for His kingdom work, rather than as my own instrument for my personal comfort and security. I had a new freedom in giving, trusting God to speak to me about where, when, and how much. Life for me literally began anew. He was starting the process of freeing me from my self and all its hang-ups!

The "crucifixion moment" I told you about in Day 1 happened during a two-day business consulting trip that a friend had set up for me. After making this gut-wrenching decision, I came home to try to explain to my family what I had done. I was a little concerned they might not understand the depth of this decision and the tremendous impact it had made on my life. At the time, our three girls were 16, 15, and 12 years old, and although they were very mature spiritually, I just didn't think they would get it. Anyway, I sat the whole family down one night with my workbook showing some of the key illustrations and began to share. It was amazing! They not only heard, they really got it! In fact, a revival broke out in our family when each person confessed how their particular "flesh" had hurt or been used against another family member. I had never seen anything like it before. Christ's life was at work in each of us, and He wasn't through yet (and He still isn't)!

Within four weeks of my job loss, the heavenly Vinedresser picked up the shears and began working on Denise and her relationship with our oldest daughter Danielle, who had just turned 17. The incredible testimony of her trip to the cross is one every mother should hear in learning how to let go of your children. God gave her a unique revelation of spiritual truth as it applies to this very difficult task. I encourage you and your wife to get the companion *Freedom for Mothers* workbook.

God provided a new job for me within eight weeks of my job loss. I wasn't out of work for long, but those eight weeks seemed like eight years! However, and I say this in all honesty, that job loss was the best thing that ever happened to us. Our family will never be the same again after the events of 1993. Did we know what was coming? No! Would we do it again? Absolutely!

Dad, is there someone or something—a job, a wife, a child, a hobby, a possession—you need to let go of in order to take hold of the life of Jesus and His resurrection power? Journal your response to Him.

Lord, I lay down my life. I let go of every person and everything that I am grasping, and I take hold only of You. I want the cross to have its full effect in my life. Here is my life. Take it and use it as You will. Don't stop using Your pruning shears until I am clean. This I pray in the name of Jesus Christ. Amen.

Signs of Brokenness

All rights surrendered

Willing to be out of control

Not believing in or living by feelings or old patterns but by Christ within

Willing to fail

Willing to be weak

A sense of total inadequacy in self-strength

Recognizing God's power in my weakness

Trusting God in whatever circumstance; Resting even with external turmoil

Seeking Christ himself more than His benefits

Forgiving of all

Willing to be rejected

Transparent—Willing to share weakness

Vulnerable—Willing to share failures

Readiness to let others receive credit

Genuine humility

Placing value upon those who have little or no value to myself

A readiness to affirm others

Teachable

Willing to be misunderstood

Willing to be broken again[4]

Notes

[1] *Handbook to Happiness,* Charles Solomon (Wheaton, Ill.: Tyndale House, 1971, 1983, 1999)

[2] Ibid, page 109.

[3] From a story told by Bible teacher, Joyce Meyer, on a radio program.

[4] *Discover The Masters Plan for Mastering Life,* Association of Exchanged Life Ministries, Inc., 1993, pp. 29-30.

WEEK 6

THE PRINCIPLE OF THE BUD: GRAFTED TO THE VINE

How a father views himself—who he is and why he is on the earth—makes all the difference in his parenting. Having a poor self- image makes for being a poor father. Having an overly positive self-image may even be worse. We fathers need to know who we are. We need to know why we are here. So we turn to God's Word.

FatherWise Group Prayer Requests

The first person in the group will share a one sentence prayer request about his wife or his children. Each person in the group will pray a one sentence prayer over that request before moving on to the next person's request. The group will continue in this way until everyone has prayed over each request.

DAY 1

A NEW LIFE

BEGIN WITH PRAYER

Worship God as the Giver of Life. Praise Him for burying your old life and giving you new, resurrected life in Him.

A man's view of his identity and purpose makes all the difference in being a dad. We must know who we are and why we're here in order to father our kids the right way.

THE TRUTH ABOUT YOU AND ME.

Let me put it as simply as I can: You were born with a desperately sinful nature, totally unresponsive to God (ROMANS 1:18). When you came to Christ, that old sinful nature died (ROMANS 6:6). In its place is your newly created nature that responds to God (II CORINTHIANS 5:17). Your new inner being, your spirit man, is a container inside you for God's life.

You may get confused about that "you" that's supposed to be good. Let's face it, sometimes we don't look like a saint. We live on earth in a fleshy body that can go on a real "flesh trip" (ROMANS 7). We mean to do good to our children, but sometimes we really mess up. Although your spirit is completely righteous (II CORINTHIANS 5:21), your mind, will, and emotions are still under construction (ROMANS 12:2). They are being changed gradually in a process, as you choose to "die" fleshy attitudes and actions.

As more areas in our lives express Jesus' life, we walk in freedom, love and joy. We exhibit the fruit of the Spirit (GALATIANS 5:22-23) more fully. Dads who have Jesus' life flowing through them are free to love unconditionally and to discipline fearlessly, firmly and fairly. When the kids see dad, they see Jesus shining through him. It's a powerful witness. That's how being a father is designed to work!

The Resurrection Principle.

The old hymn *He Lives!* captures the message of the resurrection: "He walks with me and He [literally, in a way I can hear Him and understand Him] talks to me." As a believer, the living Jesus is on the inside of you every minute of every day with His full and powerful life always available. Do you need wisdom for that big family decision or child-rearing issue? He is a living source of all wisdom. Do you need to get rid of the crushing burdens you are carrying about work or a difficulty with your child? He has offered for you to *"Cast all your anxiety on him because he cares for you"* (I Peter 5:7). Are you worn out, exhausted and frazzled? He is a constant source of power and strength. He is not an idea, a belief, a story, a pattern of thinking, or a picture. He is a person. And He is alive.

Read Matthew 28:1-20.

1 After the Sabbath, at dawn on the first day of the week, Mary Magdalene and the other Mary went to look at the tomb.

2 There was a violent earthquake, for an angel of the Lord came down from heaven and, going to the tomb, rolled back the stone and sat on
it. 3 His appearance was like lightning, and his clothes were white as
snow. 4 The guards were so afraid of him that they shook and became like dead men.

5 The angel said to the women, "Do not be afraid, for I know that you
are looking for Jesus, who was crucified. 6 He is not here; he has risen,
just as he said. Come and see the place where he lay. 7 Then go quickly and tell his disciples: 'He has risen from the dead and is going ahead of you into Galilee. There you will see him.' Now I have told you."

8 So the women hurried away from the tomb, afraid yet filled with joy, and ran to tell his disciples.

9 Suddenly Jesus met them. "Greetings," he said. They came to him, clasped his feet and worshiped him.

10 Then Jesus said to them, "Do not be afraid. Go and tell my brothers to go to Galilee; there they will see me."

The Guards' Report

11 While the women were on their way, some of the guards went into the city and reported to the chief priests everything that had happened.
12 When the chief priests had met with the elders and devised a plan,
they gave the soldiers a large sum of money, 13 telling them, "You are
to say, 'His disciples came during the night and stole him away while
we were asleep.' 14 If this report gets to the governor, we will satisfy
him and keep you out of trouble." 15 So the soldiers took the money
and did as they were instructed. And this story has been widely circulated among the Jews to this very day.

The Great Commission

16 Then the eleven disciples went to Galilee, to the mountain where Je-
sus had told them to go. 17 When they saw him, they worshiped him;
but some doubted. 18 Then Jesus came to them and said, "All author-
ity in heaven and on earth has been given to me. 19 Therefore go and
make disciples of all nations, baptizing them in the name of the Father
and of the Son and of the Holy Spirit, 20 and teaching them to obey
everything I have commanded you. And surely I am with you always,
to the very end of the age."

We have become so blasé about Jesus' resurrection. It's so familiar that we are in danger of forgetting the basic fact: Jesus died, came back to life and is still alive. Just as He appeared personally to several of His disciples after the resurrection, He still appears and talks with His disciples now. He said He'd be with us to the end of the age, and He meant it literally.

I want to ask you something. Please take a moment to really consider it. Do you truly believe Jesus was literally resurrected from the dead? In your heart of hearts, what do you know beyond all shadow of doubt about that fact?

Jesus is nearer than your heartbeat, nearer than your breath. He's alive and He's here. You're not alone. Take time now to stop and meditate on His present nearness in your life.

Lord, I proclaim that You are truly alive. You are with me; I'm not alone. I bless you and draw near to You now. In Jesus' name I pray. Amen.

TIPS FOR DAD

Share the load with your wife by offering to help your kids with homework. If your children homeschool, your wife will especially appreciate your help with at least one subject. It will encourage and build intimacy with your children. If your kids attend school, make every effort to attend school events to meet their teachers and see their work. Your foundation of support will provide the stability your kids need to progress through the education process.

DAY 2

A NEW HEART

BEGIN WITH PRAYER

Ask the Father to teach you how to walk and talk with Jesus throughout your day. Ask Him to make the living Lord more real to you each day this week.

We know that, among others, Jesus appeared personally to Mary Magdalene, Simon Peter, James, and Paul (Luke 24:1-35, I Corinthians 15:7-8, Acts 9). Why do you think He appeared individually to these four?

Mary Magdalene had been demon-possessed, and Jesus had cast out seven demons from her. She needed reassurance that He would never leave or forsake her. Just days before the resurrection, Peter had blatantly denied even knowing Jesus. He needed a time for reconciliation. James, Jesus' half-brother, had lived with Him in unbelief. He needed some family time to express his newfound belief. Paul had tortured Jesus' followers, and needed a face-to-face meeting with Jesus in order to believe. Each one had a "history"—a seedy past—and needed personal time with the Lord. Can you relate to any or all of them? In love, Jesus sought out and pursued each one. And He is pursuing you.

Luke 24:36-48.

36 While they were still talking about this, Jesus himself stood among them and said to them, "Peace be with you."

37 They were startled and frightened, thinking they saw a ghost.

38 He said to them, "Why are you troubled, and why do doubts rise
in your minds? 39 Look at my hands and my feet. It is I myself! Touch
me and see; a ghost does not have flesh and bones, as you see I have."

40 When he had said this, he showed them his hands and feet. 41 And
while they still did not believe it because of joy and amazement, he
asked them, "Do you have anything here to eat?" 42 They gave him a
piece of broiled fish, 43 and he took it and ate it in their presence.

44 He said to them, "This is what I told you while I was still with you:
Everything must be fulfilled that is written about me in the Law of
Moses, the Prophets and the Psalms."

45 Then he opened their minds so they could understand the Scrip-
tures. 46 He told them, "This is what is written: The Christ will suffer
and rise from the dead on the third day, 47 and repentance and for-
giveness of sins will be preached in his name to all nations, beginning
at Jerusalem. 48 You are witnesses of these things."

Jesus was so practical. He ate a meal in front of His shocked disciples to prove to them that He truly had risen and was with them again. He opened their minds to the Scriptures like never before. He proved that the whole Bible was literally true and accurate. Once they had been through His death, burial and resurrection, it all came together and made sense. They got it!

Do you get it? The whole point of the good news about Jesus is that He is a living God. He's not dead like Buddha or Mohammed or Brigham Young. We have a personal mentor who doesn't just leave us a written holy book to follow. We have the Author of the book personally instructing and lovingly guiding us toward the light from inside our hearts!

Are you seeing the impact of the resurrection on your daily life? Just as you hover over your child to guide, lead, protect and train him in his best interest because you love him, Jesus is hovering over you. You are His child, His precious one, dearly loved. And He has not left you alone. He is ever-present, ever-watching, ever-knowing, because He loves you.

John 20:1-18.

1 Early on the first day of the week, while it was still dark, Mary Magdalene went to the tomb and saw that the stone had been removed from the entrance. 2 So she came running to Simon Peter and the other disciple, the one Jesus loved, and said, "They have taken the Lord out of the tomb, and we don't know where they have put him!"

3 So Peter and the other disciple started for the tomb. 4 Both were running, but the other disciple outran Peter and reached the tomb first. 5 He bent over and looked in at the strips of linen lying there but did not go in. 6 Then Simon Peter, who was behind him, arrived and went into the tomb. He saw the strips of linen lying there, 7 as well as the burial cloth that had been around Jesus' head. The cloth was folded up by itself, separate from the linen. 8 Finally the other disciple, who had reached the tomb first, also went inside. He saw and believed. 9 (They still did not understand from Scripture that Jesus had to rise from the dead.)

Jesus Appears to Mary Magdalene

10 Then the disciples went back to their homes, 11 but Mary stood outside the tomb crying. As she wept, she bent over to look into the tomb12 and saw two angels in white, seated where Jesus' body had been, one at the head and the other at the foot.

13 They asked her, "Woman, why are you crying?" "They have taken my Lord away," she said, "and I don't know where they have put him." 14 At this, she turned around and saw Jesus standing there, but she did not realize that it was Jesus. 15 "Woman," he said, "why are you crying? Who is it you are looking for?" Thinking he was the gardener, she said, "Sir, if you have carried him away, tell me where you have put him, and I will get him."

16 Jesus said to her, "Mary." She turned toward him and cried out in

Aramaic, "Rabboni!" (which means Teacher). 17 Jesus said, "Do not hold on to me, for I have not yet returned to the Father. Go instead to my brothers and tell them, 'I am returning to my Father and your Father, to my God and your God.'" 18 Mary Magdalene went to the disciples with the news: "I have seen the Lord!" And she told them that he had said these things to her.

What changed Mary's perception of the "gardener?" It was hearing Jesus call her name. Jesus is calling your name...you personally. He sees, He cares, and He knows. Can you say with Mary, "I have seen the Lord?" Ask Jesus to open your eyes so that you, too, can see Him. Focus your attention this day on the risen Lord Jesus Christ.

Finally, read JOHN 20:19-31.

19 On the evening of that first day of the week, when the disciples were together, with the doors locked for fear of the Jews, Jesus came and stood among them and said, "Peace be with you!" 20 After he said this, he showed them his hands and side. The disciples were overjoyed when they saw the Lord.

21 Again Jesus said, "Peace be with you! As the Father has sent me, I am sending you." 22 And with that he breathed on them and said, "Receive the Holy Spirit. 23 If you forgive anyone his sins, they are forgiven; if you do not forgive them, they are not forgiven."

Jesus Appears to Thomas

24 Now Thomas (called Didymus), one of the Twelve, was not with the disciples when Jesus came. 25 So the other disciples told him, "We have seen the Lord!"

But he said to them, "Unless I see the nail marks in his hands and put my finger where the nails were, and put my hand into his side, I will not believe it."

26 A week later his disciples were in the house again, and Thomas was with them. Though the doors were locked, Jesus came and stood among them and said, "Peace be with you!" 27 Then he said to Thomas, "Put your finger here; see my hands. Reach out your hand and put it into my side. Stop doubting and believe."

28 Thomas said to him, "My Lord and my God!"

29 Then Jesus told him, "Because you have seen me, you have believed; blessed are those who have not seen and yet have believed." 30 Jesus did many other miraculous signs in the presence of his disciples, which are not recorded in this book. 31 But these are written that you may believe that Jesus is the Christ, the Son of God, and that by believing you may have life in his name.

Thomas couldn't quite believe that Jesus was truly alive. Jesus told him to put his hand in His spear-pierced hands and side. Then He gently rebuked him, saying, "Stop doubting and believe" (JOHN 20:27).

The apostle John gave his reason for recording these events in JOHN 20:31: "*But these are written that you may believe that Jesus is the Christ, the Son of God, and that by believing you may have life in His name.*" John wrote his record of the events in Jesus' life so that we too would believe, and that believing we also would have life in His name. Will you believe? Can you take it in? He is risen! He is risen indeed!

Lord, open my eyes to see the power of Your resurrection life. I want to know You and the power of Your resurrection in my life. Scrape away the calluses on my heart and let the truth sink in. Amen.

TIPS FOR DAD

Keep your promises and insist that your children keep theirs. Broken promises break down the trust in a relationship. Even strong family bonds can be seriously injured by not keeping your word. And Dad, they are watching you!

DAY 3

A NEW POWER

BEGIN WITH PRAYER

Praise Him for burying your old life, and for giving you new, resurrected life in Him.

Dad, if you're in Christ, let me tell you who you are: you're a new creation. Jesus recreated you in such a way that now you can contain His life. When you were in Adam, you were hostile to Christ. Warped and deformed, you couldn't contain Him. But you've been made new, perfectly suited to be a living temple that is filled with Jesus' life. You are righteous. That new created you—that inmost you—was created by Christ Jesus holy and righteous. You're no longer a dirty, rotten sinner. You're a saint created for good works.

The resurrection has implications for your past, present and future. In your past, Jesus brought you from death in Adam, doomed to hell, into life in Him, destined for heaven. In your present, Jesus is transforming you by the renewing of your mind through the process of death to "flesh" and new life in exchange. In the future, at your physical death, He'll bring you into eternity in Him to join Him as His bride.

The resurrection tells me who I am. It establishes my identity. I'm not a helpless sinner (Romans 6:6); I am a new creation wearing His robe of righteousness (II Corin. 5:17-21). I am not Jesus' slave; I am His friend (John 15:15). I am a child of God (Galatians 4:7). If I don't understand the resurrection, I miss out on the great purpose for which I was born. I was born, and then reborn, to be an "earthen vessel" carrying around the life of the Lord Jesus here on earth.

Romans 6:3-14.

3 Or don't you know that all of us who were baptized into Christ Jesus
were baptized into his death?
4 We were therefore buried with him through baptism into death in
order that, just as Christ was raised from the dead through the glory of
the Father, we too may live a new life.
5 If we have been united with him like this in his death, we will cer-
tainly also be united with him in his resurrection. 6 For we know that
our old self was crucified with him so that the body of sin might be
done away with, that we should no longer be slaves to sin— 7 because
anyone who has died has been freed from sin.
8 Now if we died with Christ, we believe that we will also live with
him. 9 For we know that since Christ was raised from the dead, he can-
not die again; death no longer has mastery over him. 10 The death he
died, he died to sin once for all; but the life he lives, he lives to God.
11 In the same way, count yourselves dead to sin but alive to God in
Christ Jesus. 12 Therefore do not let sin reign in your mortal body so
that you obey its evil desires. 13 Do not offer the parts of your body to
sin, as instruments of wickedness, but rather offer yourselves to God, as
those who have been brought from death to life; and offer the parts of
your body to him as instruments of righteousness. 14 For sin shall not
be your master, because you are not under law, but under grace.

Verse 6 states what has happened in the past: your "old self" was crucified with Christ, making you free from slavery to sin. Verse 11 explains your present "crucifixion" and "resurrection," saying: *"consider [ourselves] to be dead to sin, but alive to God in Christ Jesus."* Verses 12-13 tell how to crucify flesh and live a resurrected life: *"do not let sin reign in your mortal body that you should obey its lusts, and do not go on presenting the members of your body to sin as instruments of unrighteousness; but present yourselves to God as those alive from the dead, and your members as instruments of righteousness to God."*

Romans 8:9-11.

9 You, however, are controlled not by the sinful nature but by the Spirit, if the Spirit of God lives in you. And if anyone does not have the Spirit of Christ, he does not belong to Christ. 10 But if Christ is in you, your body is dead because of sin, yet your spirit is alive because of righteousness. 11 And if the Spirit of him who raised Jesus from the dead is living in you, he who raised Christ from the dead will also give life to your mortal bodies through his Spirit, who lives in you.

Dad, you're alive. This is why you can "esteem" or love yourself. You're a new creation in Christ. We don't need to work on "self-esteem." That would just build up our flesh, making stronger what needs to die. Instead, we need to know who we are: His workmanship, created in Him for good works. Yes, we'll have "Romans 7" struggles, our flesh waging war against our spirit. But cooperate with God, and change will occur.

Suppose a family buys a home. They love the floor plan but not the décor. So over time, they take out the old and put in the new. The home starts to reflect their character. Similarly, you've been bought by a new owner. He resides in you and has given you a completely new inner man to contain His life. He's in the process of transforming your mind, will and emotions. He's remaking you on the inside to match your true identity. So believe the truth about who you really are!

Lord, thank You for the truth that I am a new creation. Help me to know this truth that can set me free. In Jesus' name. Amen.

TIPS FOR DAD

Speaking of self-esteem, James Dobson's book, *What Wives Wish Their Husbands Knew About Women* [1], shares a survey of Christian women. The number one source of depression was, you guessed it, low self-esteem. Dad, your wife can never get too much praise, especially if she is a stay-at-home mom. My tip today is to practice praising your wife. It may not come easily or naturally. If not, begin to speak praise to the Lord about her. It will become easier to praise her openly. Try it!

DAY 4

A NEW PLACE

BEGIN WITH PRAYER

Ask the Father to transform you by the renewing of your mind. Ask Him to bind your mind to His mind and your heart to His heart.

I want to clarify the difference between who you are and who you are becoming. They are radically different things.

A NEW CREATION.

Who you are is a new creation, loved by God. You are a completely different species of man from non-Christians. They have dead spirits that cannot contain the life of Jesus. Your spirit has come alive and can contain His life. You have no excuse to feel defeated, inferior or inadequate. You simply aren't! You are a magnificent, new creation of God. II CORINTHIANS 5:17 says: *"Therefore if any man is in Christ, he is a new creature; the old things passed away; behold, new things have come."* GALATIANS 6:15 tells us that the only thing that truly matters in life is being a new creation.

ROMANS 8:10-11, 15-17.

10 But if Christ is in you, your body is dead because of sin, yet your spirit is alive because of righteousness. 11 And if the Spirit of him who raised Jesus from the dead is living in you, he who raised Christ from the dead will also give life to your mortal bodies through his Spirit, who lives in you.

15 For you did not receive a spirit that makes you a slave again to
fear, but you received the Spirit of sonship. And by him we cry, "Abba,
Father." 16 The Spirit himself testifies with our spirit that we are God's
children. 17 Now if we are children, then we are heirs—heirs of God
and co-heirs with Christ, if indeed we share in his sufferings in order
that we may also share in his glory.

Even though your body is "dead" because it still has the ability to sin, your spirit is "alive because of righteousness." You have not received a spirit of slavery but a spirit of adoption. You are a child of God. Jesus described our new life this way: *"Truly, truly, I say to you, unless one is born again, he cannot see the kingdom of God"* (JOHN 3:3). Our new life is "born again." He starts over and completely recreates us!

The best way I know to illustrate this is to think back to when my daughters were teenagers. I knew when one of them was in love. It showed all over her. All of a sudden, she started spending more time on her hair, make-up and clothes. She walked with a lilt in her step, and the everyday annoyances of life just didn't seem to matter. She knew who she was: a loved woman. That knowledge was enough to enable her to see herself as worthy and valuable. When she saw herself that way, it changed her whole perspective.

If we know who we are, Dad, we don't have to try to feel good about ourselves by accumulating possessions, looking like James Bond, or achieving career success at the expense of our families. We can settle down and get to the real issues of life. We can focus on being God's man—an empowered, male container of His holy life. We can accept our role, which is to pour out that Life into the lives of those He places around us. Our wives, our children and our world will know Him because they know us.

A MAN OF FREEDOM.

Who you are becoming is a man of freedom. Freed from the barriers within your heart that squelch Christ's life, you are being transformed by the renewing of your mind. With each passing season, you are becoming more transparent and able to display His glory. Your wife and children look at your face and see His. They hear your voice and recognize His words. They watch you work and see the work of God. They hear you pray and know that their father and the Father are one. Your children feel your touch and sense the touch of His Spirit.

ROMANS 8:12-13 says: *"So then, brethren, we are under obligation, not to the flesh, to live according to the flesh–for if you are living according to the flesh, you must die; but if by the Spirit you are putting to death the deeds of the body, you will live."*

Lord Jesus, thank You for my new life in You. Continue to unfold the truth to me. Take my heart and let it be your throne. Amen.

TIPS FOR DAD

If you have more than one child, you've probably noticed they are different! It's important to note the differences so you can guide each one in the way he's "bent." Spend exclusive time with each child to show your love and to get to know those special differences. Your job, Dad, is to learn who that young person is and to work for the Lord to develop him in the unique calling the Lord has prepared for him.

DAY 5

A NEW MIND

BEGIN WITH PRAYER

Ask the Father to flood the eyes of your heart with light so that you will know the hope of His calling. Ask Him to fill your mind with His thoughts and your heart with His love.

Today, we'll examine the first five chapters of Acts to see some of the wonderful blessings that come with our new creation status. What happened to Jesus' followers after His resurrection? We'll see that their flesh patterns were demolished and replaced by new patterns of thinking and behaving. It wasn't just for them; it's for us, too.

NEW POWER.

ACTS 1:1-5, 8.

1 In my former book, Theophilus, I wrote about all that Jesus began to do and to teach 2 until the day he was taken up to heaven, after giving instructions through the Holy Spirit to the apostles he had chosen.

3 After his suffering, he showed himself to these men and gave many convincing proofs that he was alive. He appeared to them over a period of forty days and spoke about the kingdom of God. 4 On one occasion, while he was eating with them, he gave them this command: "Do not leave Jerusalem, but wait for the gift my Father promised, which you have heard me speak about. 5 For John baptized with water, but in a few days you will be baptized with the Holy Spirit."

When the Holy Spirit would come, the disciples of Jesus were to receive power.

In Acts 2, briefly skim verses 2-4, 38, and 43. In chapter 3, please read verses 1-8. Then read Acts 4:13; 5:12; and 6:8-10. The Holy Spirit didn't creep up on the disciples in a gradual process. There was a decisive moment when the power of heaven connected with the hearts of men. It must have sounded like a tornado, because the sound was heard all over the city (Acts 2:6). The brand new creatures in Christ sat huddled together in one place. God sent a powerful wind from heaven that engulfed the room with its presence. As it pumped itself into each empty, waiting heart, something like fireworks began to go off around each one of them. They were so filled with the super-intelligence of God's Spirit that they began to process information that hadn't been there before. Where witnessing was needed, language was given. Where healing was needed, healing power was given.

Compare Luke 22:33, 34, 54-62 with Acts 2:14-36. What difference do you find in Peter? Before Jesus' resurrection, Peter was a cowering, cursing liar. In the courtyard of the high priest, he denied the Lord. But look at him now! He is preaching openly in the temple porches proclaiming Jesus to the top of his lungs. He boldly accuses the Jews of putting Jesus to death, and proceeds to explain the resurrection.

Can you believe the change in Peter? Did the crucifixion change him? No. After the crucifixion, he was still cowering behind closed doors. It was after Jesus' resurrection, when the Holy Spirit was released, that Peter changed so suddenly and completely. Resurrection power changed Peter.

Are you ready for that kind of change? Are you cowering in your present circumstance, defeated and depressed? Remember who you are and what you have! You're a new species of man, created with a capacity to be filled with God Himself. You may ask Him to fill your heart and mind with His heart and mind. You have direct access to Him. The same power that raised Jesus from the dead is at work in you.

Ephesians 1:18-20 and 3:16.

18 I pray also that the eyes of your heart may be enlightened in order that you may know the hope to which he has called you, the riches of his glorious inheritance in the saints, 19 and his incomparably great power for us who believe. That power is like the working of his mighty strength, 20 which he exerted in Christ when he raised him from the dead and seated him at his right hand in the heavenly realms,

3:16 I pray that out of his glorious riches he may strengthen you with power through his Spirit in your inner being,

I echo Paul's prayers for you. I want to look you in the eye and tell you: Dad, you can handle your marriage, your job, and the job of parenting, not because you are going to learn how to get 'strong' in your flesh, but because He's strong. You're not limited to your own strength and knowledge. As you learn to put off flesh and put on His life, you'll become a powerful overcomer. Being a husband and father will become the joy it was intended to be.

Lord, I want to be an overcomer, to live in freedom and victory. Accomplish in my life Your whole plan and purpose. In Jesus' name I pray. Amen.

TIPS FOR DAD

Use sticky notes to write love or thank-you notes to your wife. Put one on her mirror so she will see it when she starts her day. Put one on the steering column of her car. Put one in the kitchen, thanking her for the meals she prepares. Just a sentence or word of encouragement means so much. For the kids, put a note in their lunch or on their bed. Think about what they're going through and ask God for the right words to write. Our words are important (Ephesians 4:29).

WEEKEND STUDY

WHO YOU ARE

CATERPILLARS AND BUTTERFLIES. One of the ways God gave us to learn about the principle of resurrection life is the butterfly. It goes through four life-cycle stages to come to full maturity. Look with me at how the stages of butterfly life coincide with our kingdom walk.

First, there is a tiny butterfly egg.[2] Can you see the little dots on the leaf? Before we know Christ, we are locked away from relationship with God. We are in our "shells" until the time of rebirth.

Old old sinful natures—our deep innermost selves—are separated from God. They cannot have a relationship with Him.

The next phase of the butterfly life-cycle is the larvae, or caterpillar stage. The caterpillar comes out of the shell ready to begin life. He eats constantly. He eats so much and grows so fast that he literally splits his sides. His exoskeleton does not grow, so when he grows too big for it, it splits and he sheds it. The caterpillar goes through this process many times.[3]

When we accept Christ Jesus as our Lord and Savior, we come out of "death" into a new life. We emerge from the "eggshell" as brand new creations, capable of relationship with God. We are hungry to know Him. We devour everything that can feed us spiritually.

We grow and then have to shed those "skins" because they can't contain our new knowledge. Then we eat more and grow more until again, our "skin" has to be shed. We get pretty excited about being big, fat "caterpillars." We are fairly amazed at our own growth. We grow and grow until we come to the place of total commitment and we think we cannot grow any more. Then God is ready to take us to the next phase.

The third phase of butterfly life is the pupa.[4] When the caterpillar is ready for full maturity, he spits out a sticky substance, forming a pad on a branch or twig. While suspended only by a silken thread, he flips up and thrusts the clawed structure at the end of his abdomen into the pad, leaving him hanging head down. Soon, the soft structures of the pupa begin to harden and a hard shell is formed. The pupa stays motionless while dramatic changes are taking place on his internal structures. He is being changed from caterpillar to butterfly. It happens in the dark. It happens on the inside. It takes time. But the change is worth it. It prepares him to fly.

If we are serious about going on with God, growing beyond our comfort zone into His will for our lives, there will come a time when we enter the "cocoon" phase, so God can transform us. It will be a crucifixion time in which we die to the former ways we thought, believed and acted, and in which we are retooled for a new dimension in living. It often feels lonely, and we may be in the dark. It may seem that God has forsaken and forgotten us. Life may not make sense. But if we will be still and wait patiently for God's work in the process, one day we will experience life on a level we never thought possible. We will be set free.

The final stage of butterfly life is the mature, adult phase.[5] When the metamorphosis is complete, the butterfly emerges from the shell. At first, his wings are flat and damp. His body is soft and wet. Then he uses his muscles to begin pumping air into his body and wings, inflating and drying them to prepare for flight. After an hour or so, the butterfly is ready to fly off to find his mate and to begin reproducing butterfly life.

In a very real sense, the old caterpillar has died and has been replaced with a completely new life. The old has gone, the new has come. When we decide to make Jesus Christ not only our Master and Lord, but our Life, we are ready to experience life on a higher plane. Mature, flight-ready Christians emerge from the "crucifixion cocoon" with new internal equipment.

We are changed and we are free. Old thought patterns and behaviors have been replaced by new ones. Anger and frustration have been replaced by peace and love. Jealousy and envy have changed to sincere praise and appreciation. Depression has become joy. Intolerance and impatience have become patience. Harshness has changed to gentleness. It is more than trying to do better. It is more intrinsic than a step by step self-help program. Real internal change has occurred. We are ready to fly. We are ready to bear fruit.

KNOWING WHO YOU ARE. I want to encourage you to take the time to finish the following exercise. Get your Bible and trace what it says about your true identity. I believe you may be amazed at what you will find. Find the Scripture reference and fill in the blank.

MATTHEW 5:13	I am _____the salt of the earth_____.
MATTHEW 5:14	I am ____________________.
JOHN 1:12	I am ____________________.
JOHN 15:5	I am ____________________.
JOHN 15:15	I am ____________________.
JOHN 15:16	I am ____________________.
ACTS 1:8	I am ____________________.
ROMANS 6:18	I am ____________________.
ROMANS 6:22	I am ____________________.
ROMANS 8:14,15	I am ____________________.
ROMANS 8:17	I am ____________________.
I CORIN. 3:16; 6:19	I am ____________________.
I CORIN. 6:17	I am ____________________.
I CORIN. 12:27	I am ____________________.
II CORIN.5:17	I am ____________________.
GALATIANS 3:26-29	I am ____________________.
GALATIANS 4:6,7	I am ____________________.

Ephesians 2:10	I am ______________________________.
Ephesians 2:19	I am ______________________________.
Ephesians 4:24	I am ______________________________.
Philippians 3:20	I am ______________________________.
Colossians 3:3	I am ______________________________.
Colossians 3:4	I am ______________________________.
Colossians 3:12	I am ______________________________.
I Thessalonians 1:4	I am ______________________________.
I Thessalonians 5:5	I am ______________________________.
Hebrews 3:1	I am ______________________________.
I Peter 2:5	I am ______________________________.
I Peter 2:9,10	I am ______________________________.
I Peter 2:11	I am ______________________________.
Psalm 23 and 100	I am ______________________________.

I am:

- the salt of the earth
- the light of the world
- a child of God (a part of His family—not just created like the angels)
- part of the true vine, a branch through which His life can flow
- Christ's friend
- chosen and appointed by Christ to bear His fruit
- a personal witness of Christ for Christ
- a slave of righteousness
- enslaved to God
- a "son" of God
- a joint-heir with Christ sharing all of His inheritance with Him

- a temple where God's Spirit dwells
- joined to the Lord and my spirit is one with His spirit
- a part of Christ's body—we are organically related
- a new person, a new species of man able to house God's Spirit
- a son of God and one in Christ Jesus
- an heir of God since I am a begotten child
- God's workmanship newly created in Christ to do His work that He planned before the foundation of the world for me to do.
- a fellow citizen with the rest of God's people that are in His family
- righteous and holy
- a citizen of heaven and seated in heaven right now
- hidden with Christ in God
- an expression of the life of Christ because He is my life
- chosen of God, holy, and dearly loved
- a son of light and not of darkness
- a part of the holy brethren and a partaker of a heavenly calling
- a living stone that is being built into a spiritual house and am a part of a holy priesthood to offer up spiritual sacrifices with my prayers
- a part of a chosen race of people, I am royalty, I am part of a priesthood, holy and God's own personal possession for the purpose of proclaiming how excellent God really is. I have come from darkness into light.
- an alien and stranger in this world because I am different as a result of my new creation by God at my new birth in Christ
- a sheep in His pasture and I have everything I need.[6]

When your children are fighting in the back seat of the car, or your teenaged daughter gets jilted by her boyfriend, or your wife wrecks your car, or you loose your job, it's hard to remember who you are in Christ. It's so easy to focus on the event of the moment. You might think, What difference does it make if I know who I am, I've got to deal with what's under my nose!

Knowing who you are in Christ won't change your circumstances, but it can change how you look at them. It won't change the problem; it will change you.

If you are fundamentally an earthling who is trying to get the best you can out of this earth experience, then all of the above situations are going to frustrate your goal. You'll get angry and depressed, and if the situation isn't settled quickly, you might even despair.

If, instead, you are fundamentally a child of God—a citizen of heaven—who is living on the earth for a short time for the purpose of living His Life, then each of the situations mentioned are opportunities to express His life and His grace. We don't sit around trying to decide what Jesus would do in the situation, we ask Him to do whatever He wants, using our hands and feet.

My fighting children don't threaten who I am as a father. I know who I am, and I simply have a job to do to bring my children into submission and peace. The rejection my teenaged daughter is experiencing doesn't mean she is unworthy or unloved. I don't have to put up shields of protection for her. I know it is a part of God's plan to lead her to the experience that Jesus alone can meet the needs of her heart. No human being will be totally faithful in meeting that need.

The wreck on the freeway doesn't mean my wife is a stupid or incompetent failure. Since I am a son and friend of the living God, with the life of Christ coursing through me, I can comfort my wife, affirming her without judgment.

When I loose my job, it doesn't mean God has abandoned and discarded us. I know I am a sheep in His pasture and He will take care of my every need. As we listen to His voice and obey, He will lead us and guide us to His provision.

We often confuse our behavior with our identity. If I mess up, I think that's who I really am. When I know who I am and to Whom I belong, then I can see my behavior as being consistent or inconsistent with who I am. This is critical to your role as a husband and father.

When you know the truth, you won't be on an emotional roller coaster trying to use "good" behavior to please others—your boss, friends, wife, or family—so they will affirm that you are an "OK" person. You are already an "OK" person because God said so. Your behavior only has to please Him. Now you can do the right thing for the right reason because you are an all right person. All right?

Notes

[1] *What Wives Wish Their Husbands Knew About Women*, Tyndale House Publishers, Inc., Wheaton, Ill.

[2] *World Book Encyclopedia*, Volume 2, World Book Inc., 1987, p. 618-629.

[3] Ibid. [5] Ibid.

[4] Ibid.

[6] *Discover The Masters Plan for Mastering Life,* Association of Exchanged Life Ministries, Inc., 1993, pp. 37.

WEEK 7

THE PRINCIPLE OF THE FRUIT: RIPENING TO MATURITY

You want to live a lifestyle with your family of love, joy, peace, patience, kindness, goodness, faithfulness, gentleness and self-control. But there's a battle for your mind, and now you need a strategy to win.

FatherWise Group Prayer Requests

The first person in the group will share a one sentence prayer request about his wife or his children. Each person in the group will pray a one sentence prayer over that request before moving on to the next person's request. The group will continue in this way until everyone has prayed over each request.

DAY 1

SEATED WITH CHRIST

BEGIN WITH PRAYER

Take a few minutes to be still in God's presence. Ask the Lord to come into every "room" of your heart today.

THE PARADE. A boy complained that there were no clowns in the parade. His father assured him the clowns would be along later, but he wouldn't believe him. So the father took the boy to the upstairs balcony of the house behind them. From there, the boy saw the entire parade, including the clowns. What he had seen before was only a tiny glimpse of the truth about the parade. But now he had new perspective, seeing the beginning of the parade all the way to the end.

THE PRINCIPLE OF THE FRUIT: THE ASCENSION PRINCIPLE. When you accepted Christ, you were seated with Him in heavenly places where your real self resides. This is where you are. That is the ascension principle. You may be saying, "David, what in the world are you talking about? I'm very much right here on earth. My boss is griping, my kids are whining, bills are due, and my wife is sick. I don't feel like I'm seated with Christ in heavenly places." I understand, but I want you to look carefully at Scripture. Knowing not only who you are in Christ, but also where you are in Christ, can make a huge difference in living in victory or in constant defeat.

Do you battle overeating or lack of exercise? Are you often in a "flesh war" with your wife about finances? Are your children constantly in trouble? Do you struggle with keeping your family from being sucked in by the pull of the "world?"

Ephesians 2:5-6 and Colossians 3:1-4.

5 [He] made us alive with Christ even when we were dead in transgressions—it is by grace you have been saved. 6 And God raised us up with Christ and seated us with him in the heavenly realms in Christ Jesus,

3:1 Since, then, you have been raised with Christ, set your hearts on things above, where Christ is seated at the right hand of God. 2 Set your minds on things above, not on earthly things. 3 For you died, and your life is now hidden with Christ in God. 4 When Christ, who is your life, appears, then you also will appear with him in glory.

We know that Jesus is in heaven right now, sitting on His throne at the right hand of His Father. If you are in Christ, you're there, too – not your earthly body, but your newly created spirit, your "inner being." Earthy bodies are stuck with calendars, watches and maps so they know when and where they are. Our spirits aren't so limited. Your spirit is eternal and isn't limited to space and time.

So what difference does it make in practical, daily life? Knowing where you are in Christ gives you a different vantage point in two critical areas.

First, it provides a new perspective on events and circumstances. Remember the little boy at the parade? We must remember that we live on a plane above our earthly circumstances. We're not just flesh and blood limited to an earthly point of view; we're spirit beings recreated in Christ who temporarily live on earth in bodies or "earth suits." But we are seated with Christ in heavenly places and the stuff of this earth – both the irritating and the fun stuff – is temporary and passing. Most of it doesn't have any eternal significance. We need to major on the eternal and let most of the rest slide off our backs.

The second benefit of knowing who and where you are in Christ is that it gives you a new perspective on your position of authority over Satan and his dominion. Since you are seated with Christ in heaven, where He has completely defeated Satan, you no longer have to be defeated by the deception and undermining work of the devil. You can confidently go to battle for yourself and your family. Knowing you are an overcomer makes all the difference!

Lord, enable me to grasp the reality of my position with You in the heavenly places. Open my heart to the truth. In Jesus' name. Amen.

TIPS FOR DAD

Eventually your child will be hurt or wronged by a teacher, coach, or student. When that happens, ask God for a heavenly perspective before you say a word. Often, you should remain quiet and allow your child to learn character-building life lessons: forgiveness, humility, etc. The big picture of his life is so much more important than the little stuff. Spend much time in prayer and get the counsel of your wife before you consider going to the school to protect him.

DAY 2

SEEKING AND SETTING

BEGIN WITH PRAYER

Acknowledge that you are a sheep in His pasture. It is He that has made you, and not you yourself.

Reread COLOSSIANS 3:1-4 from yesterday's study. If you're watching television and something comes on that you know a Christian shouldn't watch, what should you do, based on COLOSSIANS 3:1-4? Why?

Setting your mind is a choice. Some earthly things you may be tempted to set your mind on include:

SETTING YOUR MIND ON YOUR MIND: If you do, you'll replay a disturbing event and try to "fix it" in your mind. You may get involved in morbid introspection of your own faults.

SETTING YOUR MIND ON YOUR FEELINGS: If you do, you may feel inadequate because you haven't performed perfectly. You'll likely waste untold hours being upset with yourself or others.

SETTING YOUR MIND ON YOUR WILL: Convinced you're right about everything, your pride and stubbornness may offend others. You may rebel against authority that crosses your will.

ROMANS 8:5-6.

5 Those who live according to the sinful nature have their minds set on what that nature desires; but those who live in accordance with the Spirit have their minds set on what the Spirit desires. 6 The mind of sinful man is death, but the mind controlled by the Spirit is life and peace;

The principle for setting our minds is clear. We're to set our minds on the things of the Spirit, not on the flesh. We are chosen people, seated with Christ in heavenly places. We set our minds on things above.

In your childbirth classes, did they tell your wife to get a focal point, to get a picture or object on which she could focus her attention during delivery? That's because focusing on something outside ourselves enables us to overcome pain. This is a little of what it's like to focus your attention on the heavenly agenda instead of earth's. Focusing on Jesus' face causes the difficult circumstances of earth to grow dimmer.

Matthew 16:21-23.

21 From that time on Jesus began to explain to his disciples that he must go to Jerusalem and suffer many things at the hands of the elders, chief priests and teachers of the law, and that he must be killed and on the third day be raised to life.

22 Peter took him aside and began to rebuke him. "Never, Lord!" he
said. "This shall never happen to you!" 23 Jesus turned and said to Peter,
"Get behind me, Satan! You are a stumbling block to me; you do not have in mind the things of God, but the things of men."

Peter did what came naturally. His Friend was talking about His impending death, and Peter tried to make things easier on Jesus. He was protective and comforting, but his mind was on an earthy channel, not a heavenly one. Jesus rebuked Peter for thinking in terms of the present, earthy moment instead of the eternal, heavenly perspective. I wonder how often we "protect and comfort" our children away from God's great plan for their lives. We must begin to live from an ascension perspective, setting our minds on things above, not on things on the earth.

PHILIPPIANS 3:16-4:1.

16 Only let us live up to what we have already attained. 17 Join with others in following my example, brothers, and take note of those who live according to the pattern we gave you. 18 For, as I have often told you before and now say again even with tears, many live as enemies of the cross of Christ. 19 Their destiny is destruction, their god is their stomach, and their glory is in their shame. Their mind is on earthly things. 20 But our citizenship is in heaven. And we eagerly await a Savior from there, the Lord Jesus Christ, 21 who, by the power that enables him to bring everything under his control, will transform our lowly bodies so that they will be like his glorious body.

4:1 Therefore, my brothers, you whom I love and long for, my joy and crown, that is how you should stand firm in the Lord, dear friends!

Note each attribute of the enemies of the cross of Christ. Did you catch the last one? "Their mind is set on earthly things." That's Paul's summary of their offenses. For a moment, evaluate your own wish list. Does it consist of earthly stuff? Are you investing in the heavenly places? According to VERSE 20, our citizenship is not here, so neither should our treasure be (MATTHEW 6:33).

MATTHEW 6:25-33.

25 "Therefore I tell you, do not worry about your life, what you will eat or drink; or about your body, what you will wear. Is not life more important than food, and the body more important than clothes? 26 Look at the birds of the air; they do not sow or reap or store away in barns, and yet your heavenly Father feeds them. Are you not much more valuable than they? 27 Who of you by worrying can add a single hour to his life?

28 "And why do you worry about clothes? See how the lilies of the field grow. They do not labor or spin. 29 Yet I tell you that not even Solomon in all his splendor was dressed like one of these. 30 If that is how God clothes the grass of the field, which is here today and tomorrow is thrown into the fire, will he not much more clothe you, O you of little faith?

31 So do not worry, saying, 'What shall we eat?' or 'What shall we drink?' or 'What shall we wear?' 32 For the pagans run after all these things, and your heavenly Father knows that you need them. 33 But seek first his kingdom and his righteousness, and all these things will be given to you as well."

Jesus didn't worry. His mind was on kingdom work. He knew where He came from, where He was going, and why. That enabled Him to stay focused and on task. What practical steps would help you start the process of setting your mind on the kingdom agenda?

Jesus, I choose to seek You and to set my mind on You. Show me the starting place. Pierce my heart when I lose focus. It is in Your name I pray. Amen.

TIPS FOR DAD

Setting your mind is a choice just like the radio or TV dial. To keep your mind fixed on heavenly things, remember:

1. "Garbage in, garbage out." What goes into your mind affects what comes out of your heart and mouth. Be very careful what you read, watch, and listen to.

2. Listen to praise and worship tapes or CD's in your home and car. Get CD's of Scripture and begin to memorize it.

3. Start the day praying that God would bind your mind to His will, thoughts, and purposes, and to loose you from wrong thinking, habits, behaviors, and attitudes.

DAY 3

STANDING

BEGIN WITH PRAYER

Ask God to put a hedge of protection around you as you study and to lead you into all truth.

Like it or not, you're involved in spiritual warfare, simply because you belong to Christ. If Satan can keep you ignorant or fearful of it, you'll be easily defeated. So we must take up the battle. We have an enemy seeking to devour us. But praise God, His power and authority is high above all others.

EPHESIANS 1:19-23 and 6:10-18.

1:19 and his incomparably great power for us who believe. That power is like the working of his mighty strength, 20 which he exerted in Christ when he raised him from the dead and seated him at his right hand in the heavenly realms, 21 far above all rule and authority, power and dominion, and every title that can be given, not only in the present age but also in the one to come. 22 And God placed all things under his feet and appointed him to be head over everything for the church, 23 which is his body, the fullness of him who fills everything in every way.

6:10 Finally, be strong in the Lord and in his mighty power. 11 Put on the full armor of God so that you can take your stand against the devil's schemes. 12 For our struggle is not against flesh and blood, but against the rulers, against the authorities, against the powers of this dark world and against the spiritual forces of evil in the heavenly realms. 13 Therefore put on the full armor of God, so that when the day of evil comes, you may be able to stand your ground, and after you have done everything, to stand. 14 Stand firm then, with the belt of truth buckled around your waist, with the breastplate of righteousness in place, 15 and with your feet fitted with the readiness that comes from the gospel of peace. 16 In addition to all this, take up the shield of faith, with which you can extinguish all the flaming arrows of the evil one. 17 Take the helmet of salvation and the sword of the Spirit, which is the word of God. 18 And pray in the Spirit on all occasions with all kinds of prayers and requests. With this in mind, be alert and always keep on praying for all the saints.

To resist Satan, we're to strap on the belt of truth, the Bible. Spend time daily drinking in Scripture. We're to put on the breastplate of righteousness, walking in Christ's righteousness by obeying His Word. We're to put on the shoes of the gospel of peace, hold up our faith shield to quench the enemy's darts, cover our heads with the helmet of salvation, and be ready with the sword of the Spirit in hand. Then we're to pray at all times with perseverance.

Our enemy is Satan and his demonic henchmen (EPHESIANS 6:12). GENESIS 3:1, which describes him as a crafty serpent, tells us that he *"was more subtle than any beast of the field..."* Our enemy is crafty, subtle, clever, sharp and deceptive. He caused Eve to doubt God's Word and character. Jesus describes Satan as a murderer and liar (JOHN 8:44).

The Hebrew word for Satan is spelled like the English word. It means "opponent, the arch-enemy of good, adversary."[1]Devil in Greek is *diabolos*, meaning "false accuser, devil, slanderer."[2]His agenda is to blind you to truth, make you doubt God's Word, deceive you, and plant lies in your head. If He can make you believe a lie, you're no threat to him. You'll eventually self-destruct. Your false thoughts will lead to bad behaviors and habits that trap you.

But don't be afraid of Satan. He has no power over you because you are in Christ, God's own child. Don't let Satan mess with you! Although it may seem that he has frightening power, read Job 1 and 2. According to Job 1:12 and 2:6, Satan's power is limited to only that which God allows.

As a young dad, I was challenged by a sermon based on these verses in Job. In Job 1:5, we see that Job would continually rise up early in the morning, pray and offer a burnt offering for each of his children. Verse 10 shows the effects of his prayers from Satan's point of view: "*Have You not made a hedge about him and his house and all that he has, on every side?*" There was such a hedge of protection around Job's home and family that Satan couldn't get in! In that moment, I committed to pray a hedge of protection around our family daily. Looking back, I see the "hedge" He's placed around us. Would you make this commitment to your family?

Lord, You have Your foot on Satan's neck and have complete dominion over him. You are my God, in You I place all my trust. Defeat the enemy, Lord, in every area of my life and protect my family from his attack. In Jesus' name I pray. Amen.

TIPS FOR DAD

Scripture to pray a hedge of protection for your children: That they'll...

Know Christ as Savior early in life (Psalm 63; II Timothy 3:15).

Have a hatred for sin (Psalm 97:10).

Be caught when guilty (Psalm 119:71).

Be protected from the evil one in each area of their lives: spiritual, emotional, and physical (John 17:15).

Have a responsible attitude in all their interpersonal relationships (Daniel 6:3).

Respect those in authority over them (Romans 13:1).

Desire the right kind of friends and be protected from the wrong friends (Proverbs 1:10-11).

Be protected from the wrong mate and saved for the right one (II Corinthians 6:14-17).

Be kept pure until marriage, as well as those they marry (I Corinthians 6:18-20).

Learn to totally submit to God and actively resist Satan in all circumstances (James 4:7).

Be single hearted, willing to be sold out to Jesus Christ (Romans 12:1-2).

Be hedged in so they cannot find their way to wrong people or wrong places, and that the wrong people cannot find their way to them (Hosea 2:6).[3]

DAY 4

SUBMIT

BEGIN WITH PRAYER

Ask the Lord to put a hedge of protection around your mind today.

The enemy wants to keep you unaware of him. He knows he's powerless over you, but he can defeat you if he can keep you frightened into running from the truth about him. Don't buy it. Study God's Word. Yesterday we looked at the identity of our enemy. Today we'll look at Satan's descent from heaven to hell (Sheol) after he sinned against God.

Isaiah 14:3-15.

3 On the day the LORD gives you relief from suffering and turmoil and cruel bondage, 4 you will take up this taunt against the king of Babylon: How the oppressor has come to an end! How his fury has ended!

5 The LORD has broken the rod of the wicked, the scepter of the rulers, 6 which in anger struck down peoples with unceasing blows, and in fury subdued nations with relentless aggression.

7 All the lands are at rest and at peace; they break into singing.

8 Even the pine trees and the cedars of Lebanon exult over you and say, "Now that you have been laid low, no woodsman comes to cut us down."

9 The grave below is all astir to meet you at your coming; it rouses the spirits of the departed to greet you—all those who were leaders in the world; it makes them rise from their thrones—all those who were kings over the nations.

10 They will all respond,they will say to you, "You also have become weak, as we are; you have become like us."

11 All your pomp has been brought down to the grave, along with the noise of your harps; maggots are spread out beneath you and worms cover you.

12 How you have fallen from heaven, O morning star, son of the dawn! You have been cast down to the earth, you who once laid low the nations!

13 You said in your heart, "I [Satan] will ascend to heaven; I will raise my throne above the stars of God; I will sit enthroned on the mount of assembly, on the utmost heights of the sacred mountain.

14 I will ascend above the tops of the clouds; I will make myself like the Most High."

15 But you are brought down to the grave, to the depths of the pit.

PROVERBS 16:18.

18 Pride goes before destruction, a haughty spirit before a fall.

Satan's sin was pride. He wanted to ascend to God's throne and take it! Pride caused his fall from heaven. Pause now and ask God honestly: "Is there a prideful attitude in me?" If (or when) He brings something to mind, take time to deal with it.

The power to have a victorious life does not have its source on the inside of you. Remember, He's the Vine, and you are the branch. The power for life is only on the inside of you if it comes from Christ and Christ alone. If someone tells you, "Find the truth within," they are repeating Satan's lie. The truth is outside of you and truth has a name: Jesus.

You don't have to be smart enough to make life work out for everyone! Our God is all-wise, all-knowing, everywhere-present. Take a load off. Humble yourself. Let God be God. ISAIAH 57:15 tells us that He dwells not only *"in a high and holy place, but also with him who is contrite and lowly in spirit, to revive the spirit of the lowly and to revive the heart of the contrite."*

MATTHEW 18:4.

4 Therefore, whoever humbles himself like this child is the greatest in the kingdom of heaven.

MATTHEW 23:12.

12 For whoever exalts himself will be humbled, and whoever humbles himself will be exalted.

JAMES 4:10.

10 Humble yourselves before the Lord, and he will lift you up.

I PETER 5:5-9.

5 Young men, in the same way be submissive to those who are older. All of you, clothe yourselves with humility toward one another, because, "God opposes the proud but gives grace to the humble." 6 Humble yourselves, therefore, under God's mighty hand, that he may lift you up in due time. 7 Cast all your anxiety on him because he cares for you.

8 Be self-controlled and alert. Your enemy the devil prowls around like a roaring lion looking for someone to devour. 9 Resist him, standing firm in the faith, because you know that your brothers throughout the world are undergoing the same kind of sufferings.

Do you see how pride and vulnerability to Satan's schemes are connected? So the first strategy against the enemy is this: Humble yourself! If we bow before God and give up rights to our agenda, it shuts the door in Satan's face. He can't gain easy entrance into our lives. That doesn't mean the battle is all over, but it's a good start.

True Headship. A synonym of bow, as in "bow before the throne," is *submit.*[4] That's a tough word to a lot of men. After all, isn't submission for wives?

I CORINTHIANS 11:3.

3 Now I want you to realize that the head of every man is Christ, and the head of the woman is man, and the head of Christ is God.

This verse does say man is the head of woman, but first says Christ is the head of man. Being head of home isn't demanding obedience; headship begins with submission to Christ.

MATTHEW 8:5-9.

5 When Jesus had entered Capernaum, a centurion came to him, asking for help. 6 "Lord," he said, "my servant lies at home paralyzed and in terrible suffering." 7 Jesus said to him, "I will go and heal him."

8 The centurion replied, "Lord, I do not deserve to have you come under my roof. But just say the word, and my servant will be healed. 9 For I myself am a man under authority, with soldiers under me. I tell this one, 'Go,' and he goes; and that one, 'Come,' and he comes. I say to my servant, 'Do this,' and he does it."

The centurion was "a man under authority" (VERSE 9). His authority came from Caesar. So when the centurion gave an order, his soldiers were really hearing Caesar! Likewise, a husband's authority comes not from who he is, but from who Christ is. We're not superior or more capable than our wives; we're just under orders. We must humble ourselves under Christ's authority. If a husband is not obeying Christ, his wife will find it hard to submit. Maybe our wives don't know how to submit to us because they've never seen it in action. We can set an example by our submissiveness to the Lord. Submission to Christ as an example for your wife is both an offensive and defensive weapon. It's offensive because it binds you together in unity. It's defensive because it doesn't give Satan a foothold in your lives.

God, I humble myself before You. Forgive me for leading in my own strength. Jesus, I want to submit to Your authority. Amen.

TIPS FOR DAD

On Saturday morning, watch a few cartoons. Count the number of demonic, occultist, evil characters you see. Does it remind you of the Scripture in James about Satan seeking his prey? Watch a few music videos. Listen briefly to a rock radio station. Look at TV and movie guides. Go into a toy store and count the toys with an evil seductive message. You need to know what influences are "out there" to impact your child negatively. Then strategize a plan with your wife to protect your children.

DAY 5

THE SWORD

BEGIN WITH PRAYER

Ask Jesus to teach you to stand firm against the enemy.

Today we'll take a last look at Satan's tactics, then we'll be ready to move on quickly to victory.

GENESIS 3:1-6.

1 Now the serpent was more crafty than any of the wild animals the LORD God had made. He said to the woman, "Did God really say, 'You must not eat from any tree in the garden'?"

2 The woman said to the serpent, "We may eat fruit from the trees in the garden, 3 but God did say, 'You must not eat fruit from the tree that is in the middle of the garden, and you must not touch it, or you will die.'" 4 "You will not surely die," the serpent said to the woman. 5 "For God knows that when you eat of it your eyes will be opened, and you will be like God, knowing good and evil."

6 When the woman saw that the fruit of the tree was good for food and pleasing to the eye, and also desirable for gaining wisdom, she took some and ate it. She also gave some to her husband, who was with her, and he ate it.

In these verses, take a look at Satan's tactics and Eve's responses. His first tactic was to speak, and Eve spoke back. That was her first mistake. Second, he twisted God's words, and Eve responded with an unsure, inaccurate rendering of God's words. Third, Satan mixed a direct lie, *"You surely shall not die!"* with a half-truth, *"...in the day you eat from it your eyes will be opened, and you will be like God, knowing good and evil."* Their eyes were opened, and their innocence was gone; but they were not like God. That was the lie. He was enticing her to sin, the sin of pride.

What could Eve have done? She should've refused to speak to him. Likewise, if the enemy entices you with an ungodly thought, refuse it at once. Recite Scripture or sing praise songs...simply refuse to entertain those thoughts. Also, Eve could've repeated God's command. And she could've closed her eyes! Instead, GENESIS 3:6 says she looked. By looking at the object of her temptation, she engaged her body in the path to sin. Seeing the tree was good for food engaged her "thinker." (I mean, everyone has to eat!) And a delight to the eyes engaged her "feeler." And desirable to make one wise engaged her "chooser." (Why wouldn't I choose to be wiser?)

Now she was snared with her body, mind, emotions and will, but she still could have escaped. She needed Adam's protection, but she didn't seek him. Of course, Adam was there (as VERSE 6 tells us), but he fell down in his job. God's instructions were given to him directly. It was his job to make sure Eve knew and obeyed God's rules. He should have spoken up, and she should have asked for his help. But she didn't. And when she ate, her spirit died. Now Satan could use her as a pawn to get to Adam. Do you see the progression of Eve's sin? Let's look at another set of verses that shows the progression of sin in a man's life and a solution.

PSALM 1:1-3.
1 Blessed is the man
who does not walk in the counsel of the wicked
or stand in the way of sinners
or sit in the seat of mockers.
2 But his delight is in the law of the LORD,

and on his law he meditates day and night.
3 He is like a tree planted by streams of water,
which yields its fruit in season
and whose leaf does not wither.
Whatever he does prospers.

The verbs walk, stand and sit in VERSE 1 show the progression of evil in a man's life. A man doesn't just decide to have a pornography or lust problem. First, it's a passing thought he "walks" with, mulling it over. Then it progresses to "standing" – in an adult bookstore, perhaps. Finally, it progresses to "sitting" – with a prostitute online or porn flick. You get the idea. This is what a blessed man does NOT do. VERSE 2 tells us what a blessed man does. He delights in and meditates on God's Word. Verse 3 shows what a blessed man looks like: a tree, firmly planted by streams of water, yielding fruit and prospering. That's the picture of being firmly planted in His life, in His Word!

Now let's look at Jesus Himself in MATTHEW 4:1-11.

1 Then Jesus was led by the Spirit into the desert to be tempted by the devil. 2 After fasting forty days and forty nights, he was hungry. 3 The tempter came to him and said, "If you are the Son of God, tell these stones to become bread." 4 Jesus answered, "It is written: 'Man does not live on bread alone, but on every word that comes from the mouth of God.'"

5 Then the devil took him to the holy city and had him stand on the highest point of the temple. 6 "If you are the Son of God," he said, "throw yourself down. For it is written: " 'He will command his angels concerning you, and they will lift you up in their hands, so that you will not strike your foot against a stone.'" 7 Jesus answered him, "It is also written: 'Do not put the Lord your God to the test.'"

8 Again, the devil took him to a very high mountain and showed him all the kingdoms of the world and their splendor. 9 "All this I will give you," he said, "if you will bow down and worship me." 10 Jesus said to him, "Away from me, Satan! For it is written: 'Worship the Lord your God, and serve him only.'" 11 Then the devil left him, and angels came and attended him.

Jesus set the perfect example for dealing with Satan's schemes. He flashed the sword of the Spirit, the Word of God, in His duel with Satan. In the final blow, He said, "Go, Satan!" and finished the fight with a powerful slash from the Word.

So how can you defend yourself and your family against the enemy? Just like Jesus did. Memorize Scripture, so that when you're under attack, it will spring from your heart. The Holy Spirit can bring the right Scripture to your mind at the right time. But you can't recall what hasn't been filed away!

Lord, I'm taking a firm stand against the enemy on behalf of my family. Please shield each one of us from Satan's attacks. Amen.

TIPS FOR DAD

Close the "door" to the enemy. Don't read horoscopes or allow your children to do so (DEUT. 17:2-7; ACTS 19:18-20). Ask God to show you anything in your home that has allowed Satan access to your family. Remove it. Ask Him to reveal any "progressive sin" in your life and to purify your mind.

WEEKEND STUDY

IN ACTION

THE ASCENSION PRINCIPLE IN ACTION. Do you see how the ascension principle introduced in Day 1 this week could affect you when your boss is on your back and you miss a salary increase? Or your child's team loses the ball game because of the referee? Or your wife's at her wits end with the kids?

If you are only here to be comfortable on earth, those things are really going to get to you. You will get irritable and cranky at best or blow up in a rage at worst. But if you know that you are seated with Christ in heaven and at the same time inhabiting a body for the purpose of bringing His kingdom and His will to the earth, you will see each of those scenarios as an opportunity to be an open channel for Jesus to bring His kingdom rule onto the earth.

When the boss is on your back and you miss a salary increase, you will let go of your agenda and listen to what the Father wants to tell you as you trust Him for your provision. When your child loses the ball game, you will look to see what God is working into your child's life (and yours) with the frustration. Is it kindness and goodness in the face of opposition?

When your wife is at her wits end with the kids, you will recognize that God is calling you to minister to her needs but not out of your own strength, but His strength in you.

Read II CORINTHIANS 4:7-18 in your Bible. Is it beginning to make sense? When we know who we are and where we are, we can put the events of our daily lives and the lives of our children and grandchildren into proper perspective, fixing our eyes on what is eternal (unseen), rather than what is temporary (seen). We can see them as events that God uses to produce character in us. He is training us to rule and reign with Him forever. Our time on earth is the schoolroom for our training and development.

Read EPHESIANS 1:20-23 in your Bible. Jesus' throne in heaven is far above all the satanic rulers and powers. They are all in subjection to Him, "under His feet." You can picture Jesus with His foot on Satan's neck! Our relationship with Jesus is that He is the Head of the church and we are the body. Because we are one with Christ and part of His actual body, we have authority over Satan through Christ. We are heirs with Christ. We do not have to stand for Satan's harassment and oppression. He does not rule over us. We are more than conquerors over him through Jesus Christ.

Read ROMANS 8:31-39 in your Bible. I want to revisit this passage in light of fatherhood. Paul asks, "Who will bring a charge against you? Who is the one who condemns? Who will separate us from the love of Christ?"

Satan loves to harass fathers with these three questions. It is so easy to be made to feel guilty about being a father. His charge against you will sound something like, "You are a lousy father and you'll never change. You always scream at your kids. You never discipline them correctly. You're just like your dad. You are a failure."

In answer to that charge, Paul says, *"It is God who justifies."* In other words, the truth is, you may have raised your voice in anger at your children today. You may have sinned against them. But one incident doesn't make you a lousy father. Your behavior does not make you a success or failure. If you are in Christ, you are totally accepted by God and a valuable person regardless of your behavior. You are justified.

Of course, you need to confess your sin to God and to your children, asking for forgiveness and repenting. But that one behavior does not determine who you are. Satan's charge of "lousy father" is a lie. If you are in Christ, your life is a container for the life of the Lord Jesus Christ. You are a father full of the virtues of Jesus Christ.

Satan's attacks usually give you a vague overall feeling of depression, despair, and of being a failure. But when the Holy Spirit convicts you of something, it is specific and clear. He will shine His holy light on a particular area of sin and flesh in your life that needs confession and cleansing.

The second question Paul asks is, "Who is the one who condemns?" Satan would surely like to try. He may condemn you with, "You let your child down on one of the biggest days of his life. How could you do such a thing? What a terrible father you are."

Paul's answer is in essence, "Your sin that deserved the death penalty got what it deserved! It has been paid for! Christ died for it. But now He's conquered sin and the death penalty each sin deserves. He's risen. He is all the way up to the right hand of God. He is there praying for you."

The reason Satan can get to us is that the lie he is whispering in our ear is a half-truth. We did mess up. We did let our child down and we know it. If we allow him, however, Satan will use that sliver of truth to paralyze us. We can get stuck in either a self-condemning, self-torturous mode, or in a self-protective cover-up. Neither leads to freedom. Both lead to bondage.

The path of freedom is open to us if we openly confess to our Father when we sin and walk in the flesh. Openly admit that you are a failure as a father in your own strength. But your own strength is not the power source of your life. The truth about who you are in Christ is that you have been crucified with Christ and it is no longer you who are living, but Christ who lives His life in you. The temporary flesh set-back was a behavioral problem, a sin, which is not the essence of who you are—your identity.

If Satan can't defeat you with the first two questions, he may try the third. "Who will separate us from the love of Christ?" Satan's attack may come as a whiny little voice that goes like this: "Have you noticed how you give and give and give and nobody gives back? You do all the providing for your family, and no one appreciates it. You provide food and clothes and work all day. You come home, help with the kids, do the yard work, and there is still no one that appreciates you. You need to do something for yourself for a change. You need to take charge of your life. Maybe you should just leave them and get your own life."

If you fall for that line, you will end up either in a major pity party or angry and defiant. You might even leave the very ones God has called you to serve. Or maybe you're the type person that doesn't get mad, you get even.

Will feeling sorry for ourselves or vengeance or independence solve the problem? Will everyone drop what they are doing and start meeting your needs? I seriously doubt it. Will a new, independent lifestyle meet all your needs? Most who've tried it have lived to regret it.

So what is Paul's answer? Paul reminds Christians that we are not going to live in a bed of roses. We will encounter tribulation, distress, persecution, famine, nakedness, peril and maybe even a sword. In fact, he says we are "put to death all day long like sheep waiting to be slaughtered." Then he almost screams the answer! IN ALL THESE THINGS WE OVERWHELMINGLY CONQUER! How? Through the love of our Jesus. Absolutely nothing that our families or the world or Satan can throw at us will separate us from Christ's love. Nothing. Nada.

We are loved to our absolute toenails. We are loved from the tip of our heads to the bottoms of our feet. It doesn't depend on perfect performance on our part. It depends on our dependence on Jesus. Can you see how these truths impact you as a father?

If you are a guilt-ridden, defeated, depressed, dejected dad, how are you going to rear healthy strong children? You can't! The sins of the fathers will be passed on from generation to generation. But you can stop that cycle. You can be the first generation who knows who you are, where you are, why you are and teach those truths to your children!

Read JOHN 16:33 and I CORINTHIANS 15:57 in your Bible. Christ didn't promise a trouble-free life, but He did give us the victory. REVELATION 1:5 calls Christ the *"faithful witness, the firstborn from the dead, and the ruler of the kings of the earth,"* and REVELATION 17:14 assures us that this victorious King will have with Him *"his called, chosen and faithful followers."* Now we are getting somewhere! Do you see, Dad, that you have an incredibly important role to fulfill? You are a warrior with Jesus in doing spiritual battle.

Every Christian father should know that Satan has an agenda against his child. It is outlined in JOHN 10:10. He comes to steal, kill and destroy. We don't have to be afraid of a "devil behind every bush," but we also don't want to lose our children to Satan's schemes.

Because of our position in Christ, we can pray from a heavenly perspective for our children and our wives. We can pray a hedge of protection around them. We can pray that God's will be done and His kingdom's rule be established in their lives. We can bind them to Christ and loose them from satanic influences, from their own fleshy attitudes and actions, and from the world's pull on their lives. We can pray that the blood of Jesus, the name of Jesus and the Word of God would save them, protect them and anoint them.

One more word about true headship. Adam blew it, as he stood silently by Eve in her fall into sin. Let me share a word of personal testimony. The role of spiritual leader was one I had begun to understand, but didn't implement very well in early marriage. Once God instructed Denise through some older women in how to be a submissive wife, God was able to speak through her life to me about the importance of being the spiritual leader. We changed our marriage from a 50/50 arrangement where each of us had equal say in how to do things, to Denise's decision to submit to my leadership. She said in effect, "I am not making a move unless you lead." The significance of my leadership suddenly hit me like a ton of bricks. From that point on I committed to lead His way, and God has blessed us immensely through the years.

Now, when Denise senses she is under spiritual attack she calls out to me. I pray for her and many times help her get the right perspective. God has taught me to always take her back to God's Word and His Truth. I still have so much to learn, but it is such a blessing to me and a comfort to her as I implement the calling God has given me to provide spiritual protection for Denise. As a man, this is one of the most fulfilling calls I have as a husband and father.

Notes

[1] *The New Strong's Exhaustive Concordance of the Bible: Hebrew and Chaldee Dictionary,* James Strong, L.L.D., S.T.D., Thomas Nelson Pub., 1984, p. 115, number 7853, 7854.

[2] *The New Strong's Exhaustive Concordance of the Bible: Greek Dictionary of the New Testament,* James Strong, L.L.D., S.T.D., Thomas Nelson Pub., 1984, ,p. 22, number 1228.

[3] From a sermon by Dr. Charles Stanley, pastor First Baptist Church, Atlanta, Georgia.

[4] *Roget's College Thesaurus,* Philip D. Morehead and Andrew T. Morehead, Signet Books published by New American Library, 1985, p. 53.

WEEK 8

THE PRINCIPLE OF THE FRUIT: THE HARVEST

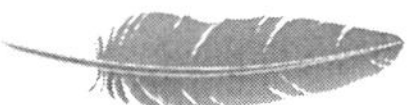

The test of knowing if you are totally free comes when you can express unconditional love to those closest to you. That kind of love is what our families and friends need, even when they least deserve it. In this concluding lesson, find the key to being a man who is free to nourish his family with love.

FatherWise Group Prayer Requests

The first person in the group will share a one sentence prayer request about his wife or his children. Each person in the group will pray a one sentence prayer over that request before moving on to the next person's request. The group will continue in this way until everyone has prayed over each request.

DAY 1

INVITATION TO LOVE

BEGIN WITH PRAYER

Ask God to teach you something new about love this week. Get still and quiet as you prepare for your study.

In this final unit, we will finish the section of JOHN 15 concerning fruitfulness that is ripening to maturity and bringing forth the harvest. Does a peach struggle to become juicy and mature? No. It just stays attached to the branch, where it receives a constant source of life-giving sap from the root. It abides.

GALATIANS 5:22-23

22 But the fruit of the Spirit is love, joy, peace, patience, kindness, goodness, faithfulness, 23 gentleness and self-control. Against such things there is no law.

It lists the fruit of the Spirit, the result of a life connected to the Vine. It's a life that receives life instead of trying to achieve it. What dad doesn't want love, joy, peace, patience, kindness, goodness, faithfulness, gentleness, and self-control exuding from his life?

And we've discovered the key to parenting our children in the fruit of the Spirit. We don't work and strain and try to achieve those behaviors. Instead, we receive His love, joy and peace, and become so transparent that when our children see us they see Him. That is what it means to be free to be the dad God designed for us to be. Let's look at the first "fruit" of the Spirit a little closer.

Big red heart. Picture a very large, room-sized red heart on the floor, representing the heart of God. If you step into the heart, you will be stepping into His heart of love. Have you ever thought what it would be like to immerse yourself in the Father-heart of God?

John 15:9.

9 "As the Father has loved me, so have I loved you. Now remain in my love."

Now we have come full circle to our empty bucket. We don't scratch and claw to get our needs met, we go to the Source. We sink ourselves down into the heart of God and draw up His love and life into us. We receive what our hearts so desired and are filled with love because we are filled with Him. There is a steady constant source of love that never runs dry, because He is love (I John 4:8). *"Whoever does not love does not know God, because God is love."*

The fruit that is born comes from the overflow of Vine-life sap. It is so full in the branch that it has no place to go but to pop out in the form of fruit. The first fruit listed in Galatians is love. Jesus said, *"Just as the Father loved Me, I have loved you."* How much does the Father love the Son? You can't even imagine it. That is the same degree of love poured out into you. Stop for a moment and drink that in. Will you receive it?

John 17:3 and 17:26.

3 Now this is eternal life: that they may know you, the only true God, and Jesus Christ, whom you have sent.

26 I have made you known to them, and will continue to make you known in order that the love you have for me may be in them and that I myself may be in them."

Jesus explains that we get the great love of God into our hearts by having Him dwelling within us. He tells us that eternal life is knowing God through Christ. The essence of eternal Vine-life is knowing God. And the result of knowing God is that the love God uses to love Jesus would be in us and that Jesus Himself would be in us. That's how our buckets get filled. We know God. We know His name, because Jesus makes it known to us. It's not our struggling and striving and begging. We know Him and love Him because He first loved us.

Are you still struggling with unmet needs? Step into the loving Father's heart with Jesus. That heart is big enough, broad enough and deep enough to fill your innermost being.

Lord, I receive Your love. Pour into my heart all the love that I can hold. I ask this in Jesus' name. Amen.

TIPS FOR DAD

In Ephesians 5, the man is commanded to love. It's not always easy to express, is it? How can we practically demonstrate love to our families? Ask God. It sounds simple, but He wants to express His love through you. Sincerely expressed fatherly love is critical in developing a child's self-esteem. When my daughter was a college freshman, she said she could tell which of her friends had that kind of fatherly love and which ones didn't. Ask God to show you how to express His love.

DAY 2

INSTRUCTION TO LOVE

BEGIN WITH PRAYER

Address God as "Daddy" today in your prayer time. Tell Him everything that is on your heart and mind.

Jesus says: *"If you keep My commandments, you will abide in My love; just as I have kept My Father's commandments, and abide in His love. These things I have spoken to you, that My joy may be in you, and that your joy may be made full. This is My commandment, that you love one another, just as I have loved you"* (JOHN 15:10-12).

Jesus had given two commands about love earlier in His ministry.

MARK 12:30-31

30 "Love the Lord your God with all your heart and with all your soul and with all your mind and with all your strength. 31 The second is this: 'Love your neighbor as yourself.' There is no commandment greater than these."

We are commanded to love God with all our hearts and to love our neighbors as much as we love ourselves. That means we have three love interests: God, ourselves and others. Jesus didn't suggest that we love. He commanded it.

The apostle John reiterates: *"And this is His commandment, that we believe in the name of His Son Jesus Christ, and love one another, just as He commanded us. And the one who keeps His commandments abides in Him, and He in him. And we know by this that He abides in us, by the Spirit whom He has given us"* (I JOHN 3:23-24).

So it's clear. We are commanded to believe in Christ and to love one another. But how do we love when we've been hurt? Wronged? Insulted? Abused? How can we keep this commandment to love?

Forgiveness. Again, Christ gives us the answer: *"You have heard that it was said, 'YOU SHALL LOVE YOUR NEIGHBOR, and hate your enemy.' But I say to you, love your enemies, and pray for those who persecute you in order that you may be sons of your Father who is in heaven; for He causes His sun to rise on the evil and the good, and sends rain on the righteous and the unrighteous. For if you love those who love you, what reward have you? Do not even the tax-gatherers do the same? And if you greet your brothers only, what do you do more than others? Do not even the Gentiles do the same? Therefore you are to be perfect, as your heavenly Father is perfect"* (MATTHEW 5:43-48).

Do you see the two things you are to do for people who are hard to love in VERSE 44? You're to love and pray for them. And there is an implied reward for doing so, according to this passage.

In the margin, write the initials of the person in your life who is difficult to love. Maybe there is more than one. Now fill in the blank: "I choose this day to love _______________ (initials) as an act of my will and not my feelings. I have been crucified with Christ and no longer live. The love of Christ is in me and that is enough to love him/her."

Say a prayer for this person. It might go something like this:

Lord, I ask You to pour out Your love on ___________. I forgive them for every hurt they have caused me and I ask You to forgive them. Bless them, Father. Put Your hand of blessing on every part of their life. Show them Your love. I pray this in Jesus' name. Amen.

TIPS FOR DAD

Many times the people we need to forgive the most in order to become a good parent, are those who parented us: our own mom and dad. There's no such thing as a perfect home or perfect parents. All families are dysfunctional in some small way or another. So it's pretty easy to be critical of the way we were raised, even in good homes. Search your heart and see if you have any unforgiveness toward your parents. Ask God to show you what you need to do to bring total forgiveness and healing in this area. Use the prayer above as a prayer of forgiveness for any hurts you may feel. Take the time necessary for God to bring total and complete healing in this important area of your life.

DAY 3

INSPIRATION TO LOVE

BEGIN WITH PRAYER

Pray for all those in authority over you today: for government leaders, for your pastor and for your boss.

No one has demonstrated love like the Lord Jesus Christ. His is perfect love. In His teaching in JOHN 15, he gives us the secret to His love: *"Greater love has no one than this, that one lay down his life for his friends"* (JOHN 15:13). And I JOHN 3:16 tells us, *"We know love by this, that He laid down His life for us; and we ought to lay down our lives for the brethren."*

RUTH 1:1-17

1 In the days when the judges ruled, there was a famine in the land, and a man from Bethlehem in Judah, together with his wife and two sons, went to live for a while in the country of Moab. 2 The man's name was Elimelech, his wife's name Naomi, and the names of his two sons were Mahlon and Kilion. They were Ephrathites from Bethlehem, Judah. And they went to Moab and lived there.

3 Now Elimelech, Naomi's husband, died, and she was left with her two sons. 4 They married Moabite women, one named Orpah and the other Ruth. After they had lived there about ten years, 5 both Mahlon and Kilion also died, and Naomi was left without her two sons and her husband.

6 When she heard in Moab that the LORD had come to the aid of his people by providing food for them, Naomi and her daughters-in-law prepared to return home from there. 7 With her two daughters-in-law she left the place where she had been living and set out on the road that would take them back to the land of Judah.

8 Then Naomi said to her two daughters-in-law, "Go back, each of you, to your mother's home. May the LORD show kindness to you, as you have shown to your dead and to me. 9 May the LORD grant that each of you will find rest in the home of another husband." Then she kissed them and they wept aloud 10 and said to her, "We will go back with you to your people."

11 But Naomi said, "Return home, my daughters. Why would you come with me? Am I going to have any more sons, who could become your husbands? 12 Return home, my daughters; I am too old to have another husband. Even if I thought there was still hope for me—even if I had a husband tonight and then gave birth to sons- 13 would you wait until they grew up? Would you remain unmarried for them? No, my daughters. It is more bitter for me than for you, because the LORD's hand has gone out against me!"

14 At this they wept again. Then Orpah kissed her mother-in-law good-by, but Ruth clung to her. 15 "Look," said Naomi, "your sister-in-law is going back to her people and her gods. Go back with her."

16 But Ruth replied, "Don't urge me to leave you or to turn back from you. Where you go I will go, and where you stay I will stay. Your people will be my people and your God my God. 17 Where you die I will die, and there I will be buried. May the LORD deal with me, be it ever so severely, if anything but death separates you and me."

Ruth had the opportunity to avoid making a sacrifice, just as her sister-in-law did. But Ruth chose to leave her family and country to remain faithful to her love for Naomi. (Read the entire book of RUTH today if you have time. It's a great short story.)

Ruth's example shows us how to be free—free to love unconditionally. It happens when you lay down your life sacrificially and choose to love; when you pour yourself out so He can pour Himself in.

Does that mean you are to be a milk-toast, weak husband whose wife bulldozes over him? No! Sometimes laying down our lives means laying down passivity. Does "laying down our lives" mean that we are to do everything our kids want so that we don't have a life? No! Sometimes it means tough love that rightly prioritizes our lives and our children's. And that means they are not the center of the universe!

What does it mean to lay down our lives? It means giving up on having "what I want, when I want it, the way I want it." It means letting go of my "right" to my agenda for my life, turning control over to Jesus and submitting my will to His.

If you're a father of young children, part of what it will mean to lay down your life will be in the physical area. You'll probably give up some sleep. You may have a little one banging on the bathroom door when you step into the shower. You may live with cracker crumbs in your car.

With elementary school-aged children, you'll be asked to give up much of your own schedule. Going to recitals, games, birthday parties, church activities and scouts will take up the time you once spent on your leisure or work.

Pre-teens and teens take all you've got. You'll take your life in your hands teaching them to drive, cry with them when they lose the game or special friend, and agonize with them over college entrance exams. You'll sacrifice new furniture for college savings and a new suit for school play costumes. You'll lose sleep waiting up for them. You'll lose sleep when they need to talk, which is rarely before midnight.

Adult children still need your sacrificial love. It may mean giving up time with them so they can be with the "other" family, or helping with a grandchild. It may mean setting boundaries to force them into adult responsibilities, not picking up the pieces of their poor decisions.

Laying down your life means being expendable in God's hand for the sake of those He's put into your life. It's signing a blank check of your life and handing it to God to let Him fill in the amount. Are you willing to pay the price?

Spend time today consciously laying down your life at the foot of the cross. In what area do you currently find yourself faced with laying down your life? Then read RUTH 4:13-22 in your Bible to see how God filled the "bucket" Ruth had poured out.

Lord, I lay down my life. I lay it down in my marriage, my parenting, my work and my ministry. I trust You to meet all my needs according to Your riches in glory by Christ Jesus. Amen.

TIPS FOR DAD

Think before you speak. Follow through. Expect good behavior from your children. Say what you mean.

DAY 4

INTIMATE LOVE

BEGIN WITH PRAYER

Ask God to teach you today how to nourish your family with love.

JOHN 15:14-15

14 You are my friends if you do what I command. 15 I no longer call you servants, because a servant does not know his master's business. Instead, I have called you friends, for everything that I learned from my Father I have made known to you.

Jesus says we are no longer slaves, we are His friends. He goes on to explain the difference. Slaves don't know what their masters are doing. But, as His friends, He has made known to us all the things He has heard from the Father. We are in an intimate love relationship with the Lord. He shares His heart with us.

Now go back and read JOHN 15:9-13

9 As the Father has loved me, so have I loved you. Now remain in my
love. 10 If you obey my commands, you will remain in my love, just
as I have obeyed my Father's commands and remain in his love. 11 I
have told you this so that my joy may be in you and that your joy may
be complete. 12 My command is this: Love each other as I have loved
you. 13 Greater love has no one than this, that he lay down his life for
his friends.

Christ's unconditional love is found in VERSE 9: *"Just as the Father has loved Me, I have also loved you." How much does the Heavenly Father love Jesus? We know that love is fathomless and infinite. That is the same measure of love He has for us. You are wrapped in His love. You are snuggled into His arms, cradled in His care like a little child.*

The "medal" of significance is found in VERSE 13. Jesus describes the expression of ultimate value and love of someone: *"Greater love has no one than this, that one lay down his life for his friends."* He laid down His life for you. He stretched out His arms and died for you because you were worth it! You are of ultimate value to the God of the Universe! What anyone else says about your value is irrelevant!

Our true identity comes in VERSES 14-15. He says of us: *"You are My friends...No longer do I call you slaves...but I have called you friends."* The old hymn says, "What a friend we have in Jesus." He is willing to be identified with little old me! The Christ, the Savior, the Redeemer Jesus, the Lord is willing to call me His friend. He tells me everything He hears from the Father. He keeps no secrets from me. We are intimate friends sharing our hearts with one another. I belong to One who loves me so.

Knowing your true identity as a child of God, with all His resources available to you, has a tremendous effect on your perspective and thus on the life of your family. As a young father, when these great truths of who I am in Christ began to sink in, it was like I had been set free! God began to teach me to appropriate His power for living and to quit trying to do it myself. When He opened my blind eyes to see who I really was in Him, I began living with more confidence as a father and husband...confidence in His power available to me.

Take a few moments now to absorb the three gifts He is giving you. Take in the enormity of his love, your value in His eyes and your identification with Him.

Lord, I worship and praise Your holy name. You are awesome in power and authority. I find it hard to believe Your love for me, the way You value me and the fact that You identify Yourself with me. Thank You, Lord. Bless you, Lord. In Jesus' name. Amen.

TIPS FOR DAD

A good father fills the role of family counselor, seeking God's wisdom to identify problems or stress. It's usually relatively easy to see the needs of the younger children, since they're more open and expressive. In adolescence, your kids usually won't be as open and communicative, but establishing good communication early will make them more open to your interest and help. Remember, the best way to know if there are problems is to ask! It's important to ask at the right time, in the right way; ask when they're alone and won't be interrupted. If you detect something unusual in their behavior, ask them about it with genuine concern. At times, all you need to do is to give them a good back rub and a prayer of encouragement. Children young and old like knowing their dad is concerned about their problems, that he is praying for them and will stand with them. It's part of the family foundation every child wants and needs.

DAY 5

INESCAPABLE LOVE

BEGIN WITH PRAYER

Pray for the other men in the class, that they'll know Christ and the power of His resurrection. Pray that their children will "taste and see that the Lord is good" as they're exposed to the fruit of the Spirit in their dads' lives.

I want to leave you with the awe-inspiring words of Jesus. Read JOHN 15:16: *"You did not choose Me, but I chose you, and appointed you, that you should go and bear fruit, and that your fruit should remain, that whatever you ask of the Father in My name, He may give to you."*

Jesus chose you! Not only does He call you His friends, He chose you and appointed you to bear His fruit, the fruit of His Spirit. When you are in union with Jesus, abiding in Him, you bear His fruit. You have been chosen to be on His team. And He has given you the game plan: It is first to "go."

What does it mean to "go?" In the Greek New Testament, the word is *hupago*, which means "depart, get hence, go away."[1] I want you to read three short stories from Scripture that contain the same word *hupago*. See if you can find out what it means from the context of these verses. In each of the following passages, notice who was asked to go and why:

Matthew 9:1-7

1 Jesus stepped into a boat, crossed over and came to his own town. 2 Some men brought to him a paralytic, lying on a mat. When Jesus saw their faith, he said to the paralytic, "Take heart, son; your sins are forgiven." 3 At this, some of the teachers of the law said to themselves, "This fellow is blaspheming!"

4 Knowing their thoughts, Jesus said, "Why do you entertain evil thoughts in your hearts? 5 Which is easier: to say, 'Your sins are forgiven,' or to say, 'Get up and walk'? 6 But so that you may know that the Son of Man has authority on earth to forgive sins...." Then he said to the paralytic, "Get up, take your mat and go home." 7 And the man got up and went home.

Matthew 18:15-17

15 "If your brother sins against you, go and show him his fault, just between the two of you. If he listens to you, you have won your brother over. 16 But if he will not listen, take one or two others along, so that 'every matter may be established by the testimony of two or three witnesses.' 17 If he refuses to listen to them, tell it to the church; and if he refuses to listen even to the church, treat him as you would a pagan or a tax collector."

Matthew 19:16-22

16 Now a man came up to Jesus and asked, "Teacher, what good thing must I do to get eternal life?"

17 "Why do you ask me about what is good?" Jesus replied. "There is only One who is good. If you want to enter life, obey the commandments." 18 "Which ones?" the man inquired. Jesus replied, "'Do not murder, do not commit adultery, do not steal, do not give false testimony, 19 honor your father and mother,' and 'love your neighbor as yourself.'"

20 "All these I have kept," the young man said. "What do I still lack?"

21 Jesus answered, "If you want to be perfect, go, sell your possessions and give to the poor, and you will have treasure in heaven. Then come, follow me." 22 When the young man heard this, he went away sad, because he had great wealth.

The paralytic who was healed, the mediator, and the rich young ruler were all instructed to take an active role. They were to move from where they were to where they needed to be to be obedient.

First, the paralytic had to pick up his bed and GO home. It was time to move. The healing had taken place, and it was time to move into God's plan for his life. In the second passage, a mediator had to go to the brother who had sinned. He couldn't be passive and still be obedient. He had to move from where he was into God's plan for his life. In the third passage, the rich young ruler had to go and sell his possessions. He couldn't hang on to his old life and take hold of what Jesus held out to him. He had to move from where he was into God's plan for his life.

The paralytic chose to go. The rich young ruler did not. Are you willing to "go" and bear fruit, fruit that will last? Will you move from where you are into God's plan for you? Has God spoken to you during these eight weeks? Is there a specific area of your life where you will have to move from where you are to get into God's plan for your life?

John 15:16 says that not only are we to "go," but we are to bear fruit that remains. Have you ever thought about the generations that will come after you? Just imagine for a moment your children's children, and their children.

If you exhibit unconditional love to you children, and they in turn exhibit it to their children, can you see the godly line forming? If you love the Lord your God with all your heart, soul and mind, and your children see that and follow the Lord in the same way, can you see the "fruit that remains?"

Never in history have children been more in need of strong parenting. Never before have we needed fathers to be full of the Vine-life of Jesus more than we do now. Will you rise to the challenge? Will you be a father in this generation who commits body, soul, and spirit to being a branch hanging onto the Vine for life?

Lord, I pray that every man that has completed this course will be equipped and empowered to fulfill the challenge we all have as fathers "to turn the hearts of the fathers to their children...to make ready a people prepared for the Lord."(MAL. 4:6, LUKE 1:17) Lord, You have told us our jobs as fathers is to prepare our children for Your kingdom purposes, ultimately preparing them for Your return. We submit our hearts to match Your heart as we abide in The Vine Life. In Your Name we pray, Amen.

TIPS FOR DAD

Simplify. Choose to clear your life of some "clutter." Say no to an unnecessary activity, or just find a place to get very quiet. Remember, adding more activities or "stuff" won't satisfy the soul. The more you own, the more it owns you! Everything either needs maintenance or insurance! Have the courage to live simply...simply depending on the Vine-life of Jesus.

WEEKEND STUDY

IN CLOSING

During our eight weeks together, we have carefully examined the different aspects of Vine-life in our study of JOHN 15. We discovered that God is the Vine where all the power of life resides. He is God; we are not. Then we looked at the branch, which represents ourselves, and found that it must be empty in order to be filled. So we spent two weeks looking at our fleshy, self-nature under the microscope to see what needs to be pruned out.

Just knowing what is wrong doesn't solve the problem. The problem has to be eliminated, and we learned how to do that by taking our self-nature to the cross where it's not patched up, it's put to death. Once we've submitted to dying to our own way, a new, resurrected life can spring forth.

We saw that the bud of new life comes as our minds are transformed. New thought patterns replace old ones. And because new thoughts are in place, they give rise to new habits and behaviors. We change from the inside out. Then we learned how to maintain a more consistent walk with God, that the first principle of the fruit is setting our minds on Him.

And in this final unit, we looked more closely at the section of JOHN 15 concerning fruitfulness that is ripening to maturity and bringing forth the harvest. Like a peach, which does not struggle to become ripe and mature, we too must simply remain attached to the Life Source and abide in the Vine.

Take a few moments to journal a prayer to God about what you have learned during this study. Above all, ask Him to enable you to abide in His Vine-life more each day.

This is my prayer for you from EPHESIANS 3:16-21

16 I pray that out of his glorious riches he may strengthen you with power through his Spirit in your inner being, 17 so that Christ may dwell in your hearts through faith. And I pray that you, being rooted and established in love, 18 may have power, together with all the saints, to grasp how wide and long and high and deep is the love of Christ, 19 and to know this love that surpasses knowledge—that you may be filled to the measure of all the fullness of God.

20 Now to him who is able to do immeasurably more than all we ask or imagine, according to his power that is at work within us, 21 to him be glory in the church and in Christ Jesus throughout all generations, for ever and ever! Amen.

NOTES

1 *The New Strong's Exhaustive Concordance of the Bible: Greek Dictionary,* James Strong, L.L.D., S.T.D., Thomas Nelson Pub., 1984, p. 73, number 5217.

RESOURCES

DISCUSSION QUESTIONS

Use these Discussion Questions and Parenting Skills to begin using what you've learned in each chapter.

Discussion Questions for Week 1
Getting Started
Some Questions to Get You Thinking

Challenge: *To start an honest, helpful and hopeful examination of your fathering skills.*

1. During FatherWise, I hope to

____

____

____

____

2. The thing I like best about parenthood is

____

____

____

____

3. My greatest problem with parenting is

____

____

____

____

4. My personal experiences with God and spiritual things so far have been

____

____

____

Discussion Questions for Week 2
Parenting Skills
Toys and Technology: Tots to Teens

Challenge: *To provide safe, age-appropriate fun for our children balanced with age-appropriate work.*

The fact that the topic of discussion for today is toys and technology says a lot about our society. Most of us can afford luxuries for our children that would have amazed our grandparents. But do all these gizmos and gadgets really deliver the promised "goods" to our kids?

Name the top five toys your child uses to entertain himself/herself. (Older children and teens have toys—just as adults do—like ipods, MP3 players, computers, and mobile phones etc.)

1. ______________________________
2. ______________________________
3. ______________________________
4. ______________________________
5. ______________________________

What is the one thing your child uses for entertainment the most?

____

What is the best thing you've ever bought your kids to play with that has produced the most positive effect on them?

____

How much time does your child spend on the computer unsupervised?

____

To provide your children with fun, consider some of the following forms of entertainment:

For Young Children:

1. More unstructured toys than structured toys—balls, blocks, boxes, blankets, dolls, tents, sand shovels, pails, water, clean paint brushes, crayons, paper, scissors. Get them outside to play as often as possible.

For School-Aged Kids:

2. Outdoor toys—bikes, skates, trampolines, jump ropes, sidewalk chalk, frisbees, balls, hoops, musical instruments.

For Pre-Teens and Teens:

3. Technological toys—controlled computer access

4. Toys to avoid—Cultic toys—ouija boards, etc.

Older children and teens often turn to structured "toys" like ipods, mobile phones, TV, movies, and computers for their entertainment. But when encouraged, some enjoy more creative forms of leisure. Girls may want to get involved in crafts and guys might enjoy making model planes or cars. Some teens are artistic and just need to be supplied with good materials to work with. We've known some kids who took up photography and became really good at it. Some play musical instruments. One of our daughters spent most of her leisure time as a teen playing the piano. All three of our kids especially enjoyed puttering in the kitchen experimenting with recipes during their teen years.

When purchasing forms of entertainment for our children, we need to stop and ask ourselves some questions:

1. Will my child use his/her imagination with this toy?
2. Will my child use his/her intellect with this toy?
3. For young children: Will my child learn to "sequence" with this toy?

4. Will he/she learn one-to-one ratio?
5. Does this toy promote family unity or disharmony?
6. Will this toy encourage physical fitness?
7. Is this going to provide good clean fun?

Much has been written about the dangers of the Internet as a form of entertainment. If your children are old enough to sit at a computer...and that is about three years old...you must inform yourself about how to protect your child from the pedophiles and pornographers that lurk there.

These "beginner safety tips" come from *Kids Online*, by Hughes. Immediately teach your children that they must:

Never give out personal information or use a credit card online without your permission.

Never share their password, even with friends.

Never arrange a face-to-face meeting with someone they met online unless you are present.

Never respond to messages that leave them feeling confused or uncomfortable. Encourage them to ignore the sender, end the communication, and tell you or another trusted adult immediately.

Be cautious in assuming that the people they meet online are who they say they are.[1]

There are some great internet sites for kids. Just supervise, pay attention, and help them use it appropriately. It's probably best, however, to get kids outside creating their own fun. They'll be spending most of their adult lives with a computer...let them have fun while they can!

Discussion Questions for Week 3
Parenting Skills
Influences that Impact Your Child

Challenge: *To use discernment in the way your family uses leisure time, from the consumption of media, movie and music products to the type of outings and sport activities we encourage.*

Do you know what your kids are watching? Are you concerned about the impact the media is having on your child? Do you have a sneaking suspicion that your eight year-old is acting like an eighteen year-old because of what he/she is listening to and watching on a regular basis? Are you confused about how to decide when a child is too young for certain programs? When should you allow your child to make choices on his own?

And what about the positive side? What good things should you expose your kids to? How are you teaching them about culture, science, geography, and the great outdoors? This is the topic for this week's discussion in FatherWise.

What are your main concerns as a dad about the media and music consumption habits of your children? What has your family found to be the best way to make responsible decisions about media and music?

What are favorite outings your family has taken to expose the children to cultural events—drama, music, art? Sporting events? The sciences—geography, astronomy, biology?

Discernment about media The skill we want to learn as parents is how to have discernment concerning media choices for the family and how to teach our growing children to have discernment regarding their own media choices.

The first step in discernment is to know the "good" very well. When bank tellers are taught to catch counterfeiters, they are taught to know what a "good" bill looks like. They know every intricate detail. So when a "bad" bill comes across their desk, they can spot it immediately. It is the same with media. If your children spend time with God and know His Word very well, their discernment about what they see and hear will become razor sharp.

But does that mean we all should throw out our entertainment centers, never go to a movie and make our children read the Bible all day? If we do, does that mean our kids will never see anything "bad?" Parents, let's face it. We cannot be with our children every minute of the day, everywhere they go, for the rest of their lives. I believe the best insurance for our children's minds is to teach them discernment.

Help is available for Christian mothers and fathers who are seeking to teach such discernment and to walk the narrow path of spiritual and moral responsibility when it comes to decisions about movies, TV and multimedia. Go to your Christian bookstore and check out the resources available.

In his book, *The Media-Wise Family*, Ted Baehr teaches practical ways for parents to protect their children from inappropriate entertainment. He also provides a guide to a child's cognitive development and at what ages and stages he should be allowed certain forms of entertainment and why. His ministry, the *Christian Film and Television Commission*, produces *MOVIEGUIDE*, a monthly published guide for evaluating current movies that can also be accessed online at www.movieguide.org. Ted's ministry website is www.mediawisefamily.com.

MUSIC What about music? There is a website you might want to check out. It's www.crosswalk.com. It is titled the "ultimate Christian music experience on the web." Of course, we have to put in a plug for our kids. Danielle, our oldest daughter and her husband Cliff, head up the Christian folk band, Caedmon's Call. Their sound is folk-pop and their lyrics are thought-provoking. I think your teens and college kids would like their music. You can find their CD's at most places where Christian music is sold and find their concert schedule and more information on their band at www.caedmonscall.com.

Discussion Questions for Week 4
Parenting Skills
Encouraging Your Child's Next Step Toward God

Challenge: *To say the words, pray the prayers, and provide the materials and events that will encourage our children to seek God on their own.*

In this discussion time, you'll get practical help in leading your child to Christ and in encouraging his spiritual growth.

What is your child's next step toward God? That is, what do you perceive to be the next step in your child's journey in walking with God? Is it to be exposed to godly influences? Understand the plan of salvation? Accept Christ? Read the Bible? Pray? Be obedient? Relate common daily occurrences to God? Stand firm under peer pressure? Follow God's direction for their life?

What scares you most about your role in leading them?

What progress in the past six months have you seen in your child's walk with God?

What is your greatest concern about your child's walk with God?

Words to encourage your child's next step toward God

- Tell the truth...about heaven, hell, death and other topics that concern them
- Take advantage of opportunities as they arise
- Don't use force or manipulation

Prayers to encourage your child's next step toward God

Pray Scripture prayers over your children. This means to take a passage out of the Bible and read it to God as a prayer. Personalize it by directing it to God:

Ephesians 1:16-23

Ephesians 3:14-21

Colossians 1:9-14

Phillipians 1:9-11

Materials to encourage your child's next step toward God

Provide your child with his own Bible

Devotional books

Christian biographies and fiction

Christian music

Events to encourage your child's next step toward God

Children's and Youth activities at church

Vacation Bible School

Christian summer camps

Christian music concerts

Christian retreats

Consider Christian school or homeschool

YOUR LIFE CAN ENCOURAGE YOUR CHILD'S NEXT STEP TOWARD GOD

The single most important thing you can do is to live in absolute surrender to God. Your children are watching you, imitating you, scrutinizing your motives and behaviors. If God is real in your life, they can't miss it!

LEADING YOUR CHILD TO CHRIST

The most awesome privilege for parents is to introduce their children to Jesus Christ and to give them an opportunity to accept Jesus as Savior. While we cannot make the decision for the child, neither should we have a "hands off" attitude. I strongly encourage you to read the little book, *How To Lead a Child To Christ*, by Daniel H. Smith, Moody Press, Chicago, 1987.

From the day you find out your wife (or daughter or daughter-in-law) is pregnant, begin praying for the salvation of your child or grandchild. (I began praying for my "grandchildren-to-be" years ago, even before they were born!)

Teach your child how very much God loves him and has a plan for his life. Help your child have an awareness of sin, that is, when he chooses to deliberately disobey. Teach your child that when anyone (including you) deliberately chooses to disobey God, they have sinned. But be careful here, Dad. Don't use this as an opportunity to use guilt and scare tactics to force your child to "make a decision for Christ" before he is ready.

Answer your child's questions about God in simple, straightforward language. When he is old enough to understand, explain how Jesus died on the cross to pay the cost of his sin. Then tell him that if

Jesus to forgive him of his sin and to come into his heart, Jesus will immediately come to live inside him. Also, he will live with Jesus in heaven someday. Continue to answer his questions and pray for him.

Wait on your child to respond in his own time. Do not hurry your child to "make a decision for Christ." You are not your child's Holy Spirit. Let the Spirit do the work of convicting your child. Just be available to the Lord to be used as a vessel in God's hand to speak at the right time and to be silent at the right time.

Little children want to please. Don't use "making a commitment to Christ" as a way for your child to please you. When children know the truth about sin, heaven, hell, death, Christ's love, and His plan to pay for our sins, they can, and many do, respond on their own to Christ. I am seeing children, who are very young, understand and respond to the gospel.

When he is ready to make the decision to become a Christian, don't put it off. Don't wait to talk to a minister. Lead him to Christ in that moment when his heart is tender and ready.

Pray a simple prayer, letting him repeat. You might have him pray,

"Lord Jesus, thank you for loving me. I know I am a sinner and I need you. Thank you for paying for my sins by dying on the cross. Please come into my heart now. I want to be your child. I give you my whole life. In Jesus holy name I pray. Amen."

Then have him pray whatever is on his heart. Don't help him with the second part of the prayer. It is very important that he pray on his own, expressing himself to God. Then tell him the angels are rejoicing in heaven because now he is God's child!

Encouraging your believing child

If your child is a born-again believer in Jesus Christ, you have the awesome privilege of helping him throughout his life in taking his next step in walking with God.

While they are living at home, you have direct influence over their:

church attendance

Bible training

encouraging their prayer life

relating daily life occurrences to God and His Word.

When they leave your home, you still have a big job, Dad.

Your work is to pray continuously for your child.

Invite them to events that will inspire them.

Occasionally provide materials to stimulate their spiritual growth.

If your relationship allows, ask them questions about what God is currently teaching them.

Keep your mouth shut most of the time and pray, pray, pray.

These are questions to ask yourself if your children are still at home.

How often does your child attend church?

Why or why not?

What sort of Bible training is your child receiving?

When does your child hear you pray?

When do you pray with your child?

Do you ever hear or know that your child is praying?

At our house, some of the most important times of encouraging our children's spiritual growth has come in the every day occurrences of life. When our children are in a crisis — like losing a friend, doing poorly in school, not making the team, being rejected by peers, or making a foolish mistake — we try to listen, talk it through, and ask ourselves and our child what God is trying to communicate to us through this event. Then we pray with our child right then as openly and honestly as we know how. During these times, we learn more about our kids and more about God. It is a "next step toward God" for all of us.

Discussion Questions for Week 5
Parenting Skills
Communicating With Your Child

Challenge: *To keep the lines of communication open through connecting with your child in timely, sensitive interaction.*

At every age and stage of parenting, we communicate with our children. From the day they are born to the day we take our last breath, we want to have great communication with our kids. But how can we talk in a way they will listen? How can we listen and really hear their hearts? When are we sure that the important messages we are sending are getting through?

How would you describe the quality of communication in your family? Hot? Cold? Lukewarm?

What is the best time to communicate with your child?

What is the best place to communicate with your child?

When do you have difficulty with communication?

Do you have more trouble talking or listening?

Does your child have more trouble talking or listening?

In a perfect world, what would the present and future communication with your child look like?

The development of language through the listening and talking that occurs in family conversation is one of the most important building blocks of learning. In fact, the better kids are at using spoken language, the more successful they are in learning to read and write, and the better they will function in school and work. With that kind of motivation for communication, we want to make our family conversations meaningful. But how?

Dinner Table Talk

Dad, it's so important to have a family dinner time. It may require sacrifice on your part to be home in time for dinner with the family, but the pay-off is well worth it. For most families, this is the only time of the day when the family makes eye contact and has conversation. This is the hour when you'll get to send messages of love and appreciation to your wife, get know your kids as you hear about their daily events, express interest in their activities, and you'll be able to invest your values into them. Nothing else that I know does all that in such a short time.

Use the time at the evening meal to look each child in the eye and ask about their day. Ask specific questions about classes they are taking or activities in which they are involved. Turn off distractions, like the television and loud music, and focus the conversation with each family member. Avoid unpleasant subjects like nagging about unfinished tasks, dealing out punishment for misbehaviors and hashing out problems.

Encourage your children to swap stories, talk about what they are reading or share the best part of their day. Brainstorm answers to questions like, "What do you think the world will be like in 20 years?" Talk about current events in the news. Include even the youngest members of the family in conversations by allowing them to share an event from their day and teaching them to listen quietly to others without interrupting.

Bed Time

Sit down on the bed beside your child and chat before bedtime. This is especially effective with kids between the "little child stage" and the teen years. Most middle school girls and some guys respond to this invitation.

You will have to sacrifice your sleep to have good communication with most teens. The most meaningful conversations I've had with my teens and young adults are after midnight.

With young children, even babies, speak with gentleness and love, but don't always use baby talk. Baby talk is fine when expressing love and affection. But when you are teaching them the names of objects and giving simple directions, use the correct names of objects and events.

Be specific when giving directions to your children. Instead of "clean your room" say, "Please pick up the toys and clothes off the floor and put them in the drawers where they belong."

Play board games or work puzzles as a family to stimulate times of conversation.

In the car, play games like "I Spy" with license plates and road signs to get the family talking.

With teenaged daughters, make an appointment for a "Coke date" in the afternoon and find a quiet place to sip and talk. You might take your teen son to a good steak house or fishing hole for casual conversation.

These ideas are just starters. Brainstorm with your group about ways to get your family talking!

Discussion Questions for Week 6
Parenting Skills
Setting Appropriate Boundaries

Challenge: *To clearly set and enforce age-appropriate boundaries for our children in the areas of attitude, behavior, speech and work.*

We have a big job. The work of parenting is vast in its scope. But one of the most critical arenas of parenting is that of establishing boundaries for our children and enforcing those boundaries. Wise parents discipline their children according to God's standards. But how do we practice it? This is the topic for today's discussion.

What area of discipline and boundary setting gives you the most challenge?

Getting your child to obey? Getting your child's respect? Establishing bed times? Curfews? Food and clothing choices? Manners? School and house work? Choice of friends? Attitudes? Entertainment?

Why do you think you struggle with that area?

List some age-appropriate boundaries for each of your children.

Child 1:

____

____

Child 2:

____

____

Child 3:

____

____

Child 4:

____

____

BOUNDARY NUMBER ONE:

Take authority over your child while he still depends on you. He or she must obey you. It is your job to set that boundary and to enforce it. This boundary is based on EPHESIANS 6:1.

BOUNDARY NUMBER TWO:

Children must respect their parents. Honoring parents starts with an attitude and proceeds to action. This boundary is based on EXODUS 20:12.

BOUNDARY NUMBER THREE:

Children must relate to others in an acceptable manner. These boundaries have their foundations in the last five of the Ten Commandments in EXODUS 20: 3-17 and the further explanations of them by Jesus in MATTHEW 5-7.

BOUNDARY NUMBER FOUR:

Children must follow the boundaries set that are unique to your family. These include decisions about bedtimes, curfews, eating and dressing habits, cleanliness, entertainment, friends, church attendance and acceptable attitudes.[1]

Your child will learn his boundaries when he receives consequences for operating outside the boundaries, when he takes ownership or responsibility for his own actions, and when he deals with the boundaries of others.[2]

Part of training a child to understand his boundaries is establishing and enforcing clear, fair, appropriate boundaries for your child, and part of his understanding of boundaries comes as you become a boundary for your child.[2]

Age-appropriate boundaries.

Many parents ask us, "What can I expect of my child? How do I set standards and boundaries that are age-appropriate?" While no two children are alike in their growth and maturity rate, some very basic guidelines are helpful if you won't get legalistic about them! Remember, God made your little Suzy or Johnny unique. These are some boundaries for young children to school aged kids based on an excellent resource for parents, *Baby and Child Care for Christian Parents*, by Grace Ketterman and Herbert Ketterman.[3]

Sometime in the first year to year and a half, most children can learn to accept limits and obey your simple, clear instructions. They can learn to avoid dangerous situations. However, children under two need constant adult supervision. It is inconvenient and tiresome, but it is what is right for your child. This is the time for some serious bonding with your little one. Relax and enjoy it because before you know it, you'll have to make an appointment to spend time with him.

Between two and three, children can learn to pick up their toys with some help. He can obey your instructions if you make them simple. He will more often stay within the boundaries you set for him if he faces immediate, consistent consequences. During this stage a child learns to use the toilet, dress himself, play within safe limits, and begin to be considerate of others. He can be a big "helper" for Mom and Dad.

By the time he is four to five, most children can button, zip and tie on their clothing and shoes. They can eat with fewer messes. Most of them have the ability to be cooperative in a group, as they can submit their personal wishes to larger group's agenda. Since children at this stage are very trusting, they need help in knowing who they can trust and who they cannot.

To preschool or not to preschool is a major concern for many parents. Take it to the Lord in prayer first! Ask the Lord for wisdom and discernment. Get counsel from godly parents in your church.

Then take an honest look at the maturity level of your child. Does he obey your simple instructions? Could he take instructions from a teacher? Can he focus his attention and sit still for short periods of time, or is he "all over the place?" Does he still need long afternoon or morning naps? Do you have an eager beaver who talked early and whose mind is a little sponge? Do you have a quiet little one who loves to be home with Mom or Dad and hates crowds and noise?

Look at your financial picture. Can you afford private school with tuition and uniforms? Would it be best to home school up to a certain point?

We went through all those scenarios with each of our children. We did different things with each one, because each situation was unique. It is a big decision, but Dad, it's not life and death. Whether or not they go to preschool will not usually decisively alter the course of their lives!

When children enter school, they enter a new world. They have a new adult authority figure every year, they are in a competitive peer environment and want to please their parents with school success. If you have a school-age child that does not know basic obedience and responsibility, start now. Set clear boundaries and enforce them.

Many school-aged children respond to charts that help them develop responsible habits. Often the chart is placed on the refrigerator and stars or stickers are used to reward success for each task accomplished. We suggest having not only a "chore chart" but also an "attitude chart."

The teen years bring new challenges in setting boundaries. These years become a balancing act for you as you begin the process of letting your child have more responsibility and fewer directives from you. The goal is to send your youngster out into the world equipped to take over his life with maturity and responsibility.

I suggest that you and your wife set up a Family Boundary Agreement form on your home computer. Put appropriate categories to fit your family. If you have a compliant teen, you may want to whittle the list to only a few important points. If you have a very belligerent teen, trim the list to only the battles that you are willing to fight and win. Some suggested categories would be curfew, cleaning their room, help with house cleaning, school work, church attendance, allowances (what they receive and what they pay for), and maybe most important attitudes towards their siblings and to you as parents. It is also important to include the appropriate penalties for breaking any portion of the agreement.

Ask your teen to fill out the form by a set time. Review the form with your spouse and be prepared to compare your own completed form with your teen's.

Set a time for an appointment with your teen and spouse when everyone can be relaxed, comfortable, focused and not rushed. Listen without comment as your teen describes what he thinks his boundaries should be regarding each item.

Clarify his comments without judgment on whether or not you agree. For now, you're just listening. Thank him for his time and input and tell him you will get back to him when final decisions are made.

Spend time in private with your spouse talking carefully through each boundary you will set. When you have the final list, put it in writing and call another meeting to discuss it with your teen. You may be surprised at the wisdom your teenager might display if you give him an opportunity to have input in setting his own boundaries. Remember, your ultimate goal for him is that he will set internal boundaries for himself and abide by them by the grace of God.

There are many great resources for parents today. If your wife hasn't taken the MotherWise courses *Wisdom for Mothers* and *Freedom for Mothers*, you might encourage her to order the materials online at www.motherwise.org (or in the US by phone at 1-888-272-6972). Also, look on the shelves of your local Christian bookstore for resources to help you learn to set boundaries and discipline your child.

Discussion Questions for Week 7
Parenting Skills
Family Devotions

Challenge: *To commit yourself to a season of meaningful, workable family devotions.*

We often want to get the family together to have meaningful devotions, but many times, the reality is far from our dream.

What is your goal for family devotions?

Growing up, what did you like or dislike about the devotions your family did or did not have?

What will be the greatest challenge you face in trying to establish or maintain family devotions?

Some points to remember are:

1. Make a rock solid commitment to your family time. Be creative as you work around your challenges. Don't let illness or fatigue keep you from Family Night. Dad, as the spiritual leader of the home, it is crucial that your family senses and sees your complete commitment to this important family time together. Don't give up...it's worth it!
2. Keep it light-hearted and fun for at least 75% of the time. Start with the fun stuff.
3. Use variety in the places you eat – try the backyard, living room, out to eat, bedroom, or by the fireplace (if you have one).
4. If the kids suggest something unique for Family Night, let them lead. Go along with their plan, if at all feasible.
5. Get each of your children their own copy of the Bible, and get

same version for everyone in the family.

6. Form a circle with the family when it's time to share and talk about spiritual things. Each person needs to be able to see the others.

7. Keep a folder in the file cabinet or on the computer for Family Night ideas. Keep your eyes open to new ideas. These will come at odd moments, so have a place to store them for future reference. You may find great stories in Christian magazines that would be a good opener for family discussion.

Name your family devotions. Ours was called "Family Night." You might name yours something else. But it needs designation. When the name is mentioned, it should evoke memories in each family member's mind. Have a theme song. We had several. They were *Open Our Eyes, Lord, This Little Light of Mine,* and *Jesus, I Adore You.* We sang them for years as a family. It brings great memories when I hear them because I envision three little girls' faces shining in candlelight sweetly singing the melodies. Family time is a way to communicate to our children concepts like: "We belong to one another. We're in this together. We can face anything if we face it as a united group. You are a part of something special."

To prove the importance of "Family Night" in our home, when my youngest daughter was sixteen years old I asked her what was the one thing we did as parents that really meant a lot to her, where we "hit a home run" as parents. She thought for a moment and said, "Dad, it was Family Night." When I asked why, she said it was because of the open communication we had and the family oneness it created. She appreciated our "realness" and our willingness to show our weaknesses and to seek their prayer support. By beginning early with our girls, even when the teenage years came, they were willing to have a "share and prayer" session. We shared the real problems each was dealing with in their lives. God built "spirit oneness" in us as we lifted up these problems in prayer each week.

Discussion Questions for Week 8
Parenting Skills
Making Memorable Moments
(and Recording Them)

Challenge: *To create meaningful times for our families and to document them in an easy, accessible format.*

Most of us have stacks of pictures that aren't in albums and samples of our children's art wrinkled under mounds of magazines. How do we create happy "Kodak moments" for our families and then capture them for posterity? How do we handle family traditions at birthdays, holidays, or other special occasions?

What one legacy of memory do you want to leave with your children or grandchildren?

What is the best family memory from your childhood?

What tradition does your family observe regularly?

What memory-making moment would mean the most to your spouse and children?

How have you solved vacation and holiday hassles in a creative way?

Memorable moments with your family can be as simple as watching a sunset or as elaborate as a long family vacation. I suggest that you ask your family what memories they have from your family get-togethers and make this a dinner time conversation starter to see what you learn from each family member.

Then ask how each person would like to save those memories. Do they like to look at pictures? Can the family invest in a video camera? Do they want to draw pictures or write stories? Would they like to make a digital recording and burn a CD of a happy memory some night at dinner?

Some families love to invest time and money into projects that preserve the family memories. Others like to keep pictures in a box for simple filing. How do you like to keep memories?

One way our extended family created a lasting memory and recorded it was at one particular Thanksgiving holiday. Denise's eighty-five-year old grandmother was very alert and spunky. We created a "set" with some wicker chairs and plants, gathered her great-grandchildren, and turned on the video camera. Denise "interviewed" her so she would start telling her stories. She had a phenomenal memory and could even remember an incident that happened when she was two years old.

She began to weave her tales of coming from Kentucky with her family of ten in a covered wagon all the way to Texas. She told us about Indians who came to their homestead and scared them to death. We all sat spellbound as she remembered events we had only read about in our history books. We will never forget that holiday. Now that she is gone, we have the videotapes to replay and pass on to our grandchildren!

If you're like me, the family vacations seem to be one of the more memorable events in the life of the family. These are moments when we dads can have a lot of influence. Because so much concentrated time is spent together, the family vacation really is a time that should be carefully planned and prayed through with the entire family.

Speaking as an older father with the children out of the house, my sincere advice is to make the effort in time, money, and film to make the vacation one that brings back wonderful memories for the whole family. And when I say money, I don't mean blow the budget; but do put something in the budget so priority will be given to this important time together. The importance is not in how much money you spend, but on the quality, fun time you spend together as a family. Trust me, it's worth it!

NOTES

[1] *Kids Online-Protecting Your Children in Cyberspace,* by Donna Rice Hughes, Fleming H. Revell, a division of Baker Book House Company, 1998, p. 47.

[2] *Boundaries with Kids*, Dr. Henry Cloud and Dr. John Townsend, Zondervan Publishing House, 1998, p. 10.

[3] *The Complete Book of Baby and Child Care,* Brace H. Ketterman, M.D. and Herbert L. Ketterman, M.D., Fleming H. Revell, 1982, pp. 378, 379.